4.00

HISTORY OF THE NEW TESTAMENT IN PLAIN LANGUAGE

Also by Clayton Harrop

The Letter of James

HISTORY OF THE NEW TESTAMENT IN PLAIN LANGUAGE

Clayton Harrop

WORD BOOKS
PUBLISHER
WACO, TEXAS

A DIVISION OF
WORD, INCORPORATED

Library of Congress Cataloging in Publication Data

Harrop, Clayton K.
  History of the New Testament in plain language.

  Bibliography: p.
  Includes index.
  1. Bible. N.T.—History. I. Title.
  BS2315.H33 1984   225.4'09   84-17384
  ISBN 0-8499-0432-3

Printed in the United States of America

Scripture quotations designated KJV are from the Authorized or King James Version of the Bible.
Quotations from the Revised Standard Version of the Bible (RSV), copyright 1946, 1952, © 1971, 1973 by the Division of Christian Education of the National Council of the Churches of Christ in the U.S.A., are used by permission.
Quotations from The New English Bible (NEB), © The Delegates of The Oxford University Press and The Syndics of The Cambridge University Press, 1961, 1970, are reprinted by permission.
Quotations from the New American Standard Bible (NASB) are copyright © 1960, 1961, 1963, 1968, 1971 by The Lockman Foundation.
Quotations from the New International Version of the Bible (NIV), published by The Zondervan Corporation, are copyrighted © 1973 by New York Bible Society International.

To Shirley, my wife

with love and appreciation

Contents

Introduction

Future historians will use many terms in an effort to describe the twentieth century. The scene has shifted so many times that no one word will characterize what has taken place. This is even true in the field of religion. Churches have been involved in many different issues. Some of these were major concerns for a brief period of time, but were pushed aside when another issue came to the center of attention. But one thing that must be noted is that the twentieth century has seen the multiplication of translations of the Bible, and especially of the New Testament. Up to the close of the nineteenth century, only one translation, or at most two, was in common use in the English-speaking world. Everyone knew the Bible in the same form. When Christians conversed about the Bible, all stood on the same ground. This is no longer true. If a group gathers for the study of the Bible, it is likely that several different translations will be in the hands of the participants. And, in the process of study, someone may remark: "But my Bible does not sound like yours." Or, "Your Bible has a verse in it that does not appear in mine." It would be easy to note the multitude of differences in Bible translations, but undoubtedly the reader is quite well aware of this. And the question may well be asked, "Why?" What is the basis for the differences in translations? Does this call into question the reliability and authority of the Bible? What translation should I use?

Such questions as the above constitute the justification for this book. In past generations, such questions might be asked only by scholars in the field of New Testament study. But today laypeople are beginning to ask such questions. Although many books have been written on the subject of the text of the New Testament and the history of the development of the New Testament, most of these have been written for scholars or university and seminary students. Scholars often have the habit of writing for other scholars. Such books are essential, but they are of limited value for most of us. We cannot understand them, and we do not have the patience to struggle through them. Books for theological students assume certain background knowledge that most of us do not possess. And, while there are excellent books for these groups of people, they do not help the rest of us. It is true that we may depend upon our pastors and other leaders to give us the information we desire on these subjects, but many of us want to study on our own. We want to read, to explore, to investigate. We would like to come to some conclusions for ourselves. This book is designed for such inquiring persons. Hopefully, it will lead the inquisitive individual along a constructive path toward a better understanding and deeper appreciation of God's message to us.

The New Testament Text

In our study, we will be considering only the text of the New Testament. If one were to attempt to treat the entire Bible, the resulting work would become too lengthy and involved. In addition, the greatest changes in the last 450 years have been in the New Testament text.

But why should it be necessary to study the text of the New Testament? Have we not had it in exactly the same form through all the centuries? The answer to the second question is quite simple. The New Testament text accepted by most scholars today differs in many ways from the one developed in the sixteenth century. One cannot speak of *the* New Testament text prior to 1516. Although many manuscripts were in existence, there was no uniformity among them. A true text had to await the invention of printing and the work of scholars in the study and evaluation of manuscripts.

But we also asked why it is necessary to study the text of the New Testament. Several factors contribute to this necessity. One of these is that we do not have the original copies of the New Testament writings. It is likely that all of the New Testament writings were at first written on papyrus. This is a fragile material, and it does not last for any great length of time unless it is kept in a very dry place. It wears out quickly with continued use. As copies were made of the originals and they became quite worn, they were probably thrown away. No one thought of them as being of special value, since they had copies that were in better condition. It is possible that some of the original copies were destroyed during the times of persecution that came upon the church in the second century. Therefore, we have today only copies that are far removed from the writing of the books themselves. There are no manuscripts containing substantial portions of the New Testament that date within one hundred years of the original writings.

A second factor is that none of the original copies of the New Testament books are likely to be discovered. Although this is possible in the light of other discoveries that have been made in recent years, it is not probable. And even if such an ancient manuscript should be recovered, it would be impossible to state with assurance that it was *the* original copy. Therefore, we must accept the fact that we will have to work with copies far removed from the originals themselves.

A third factor is that printing was unknown in ancient days. Today we are accustomed to having materials printed in large quantities. Thousands of copies of a book can be printed in a short time and every one of those copies is the same. Since the last one printed will read the same as the first, it makes no difference whether or not you possess the first copy. However, the same does not hold true with regard to the copying of manuscripts before the invention of printing in the fifteenth century. Each manuscript had to be copied by hand. It was a laborious and time-consuming process and led inevitably to mistakes. No scribe could copy a manuscript without error. Certainly in our modern day, we know that it is almost impossible for us to copy a long piece of material accurately, even when it is printed clearly before our eyes. It was much more difficult for the scribe in ancient times, who was copying handwritten material from papyrus or leather. Many times the script would not be completely legible. Working conditions were often poor. Lighting was bad.

Furthermore, the men who copied the New Testament writings in the earliest decades were not trained scribes. After Christianity became the state religion of the Roman Empire in the early fourth century, skilled scribes could be employed to copy manuscripts of the New Testament. But by that time, many changes had already taken place in the text. Sometimes a manuscript was copied by a single individual. He might copy from one or from a variety of manuscripts. At other times, copies would be made in a "publishing house." This involved a group of scribes, often slaves, copying what was read to them by another slave. Obviously, their inability to see the actual manuscript would lead to the possibility of error. After a manuscript was copied, it might be corrected by the original scribe or someone else at a later time.

This helps to explain why no two of the thousands of Greek manuscripts of all or part of the New Testament are identical. Each one differs from every other one. Sometimes the differences are small; sometimes they are large—but they all differ. Therefore, we cannot take two of them and say that, since they are the same all the way through, they preserve the correct text of the New Testament.

A fourth factor is that when many of the changes were made in the New Testament text, apparently no one looked upon the writings as Scripture. The early Christians already had a sacred book, the Old Testament. They had no interest in another. Therefore, while the writings we know as the New Testament were considered important—significant enough to go to the great expense of copying—they were not placed on an equal level with the Old Testament at first. Thus, if changes were made while copying them, no one was greatly concerned. It would be different, of course, when they were later looked upon as Scripture, equal or superior to the Old Testament.

Is there one manuscript of the New Testament that we can look on with confidence as containing the exact form in which the New Testament was originally produced? Since no manuscript of a sizable portion of the New Testament can be dated much earlier than A.D. 200, it does not appear likely that any of them can be expected to reproduce the original exactly.

Someone may argue at this point that surely God would not allow such differences to exist. Since he inspired the writing of the New Testament, it would seem logical that he would also assure that it would be preserved in its original form. But that is an attempt to force God into our mold of thinking. There can be no serious question about the hand of God being at work in the preservation of the Bible. The fact that it has been preserved in spite of the many attempts of man to suppress it throughout history is a clear evidence of his concern. On the other hand, God has never promised to protect man from his own failures and mistakes. If a scribe accidentally or purposefully changed the reading of a passage, there is no reason to assume that God would overrule that change so that the work of the scribe would be suppressed. The obvious presence of so many manuscripts, each different, shows that God did not prevent changes from taking place.

Does the differences in manuscripts mean that the text of the New Testament is in utter chaos? On the surface this may seem to be true, but fortunately it is not. Over 450 years have passed since the first publication of the printed Greek text of the New Testament. During that time, the science of textual study has developed to the extent that most scholars would agree that today we have, for all practical purposes, the text of the New Testament as originally set down by the authors. There are still some places where doubt exists, but they are all of minor importance. Not a single one of the questionable passages affects any major doctrine of our faith. God has been at work in the preservation of his Word. He has not done it in a way that many would have expected. But he has been at work nevertheless. And we can be confident that the text used for the translation of the New Testament in our modern day agrees at all major points with the text as originally written nineteen hundred years ago.

The first part of our study will be to investigate the history of the New Testament text. As a background to that, we shall take a brief look at the materials used in writing in the ancient world. Then we shall consider the major witnesses to the text of the New Testament, both in Greek and in other languages. The history of the printed text will be followed from the earliest attempt to the present day. We shall consider how scribes worked and the types of errors to which they were subject. In the late nineteenth century, a method of textual study was developed that has been most influential since that time. We shall look at that method and the modifications made in it during this century. Finally, we shall see how textual study is carried out by the examination of some sample passages in the Gospels, Acts, and Paul's letters.

The New Testament Canon

A second major area of interest involves which books should be in the New Testament. This may sound like a strange question at first. However, we know that the official Roman Catholic versions of the Bible contain some books which Protestants do not look upon as Scripture. These are called the Apocrypha and are books penned between the writing of the Old Testament and the New Testament. They are found in the Greek translation of the Old Testament (the Septuagint) but not in the Hebrew Old Testament. The same situation has never prevailed with the New Testament. Since many Christian writings were available in the early centuries of the church, why were some included in our New Testament and why were others excluded? In other words, how did we get the present New Testament?

One idea that some might suggest is that God dropped the New Testament down from heaven, intact at one time. It would then follow that man had no part to play in its selection and arrangement. Everything we know about the history of the early church says that this idea has no sound basis. A second and much more common idea is that the New Testament came into being as a result of the action of some church council. We shall need to investigate whether there is any evidence to support this position.

Two chapters will be devoted to the study of the collection and selection of the Christian writings which now make up our New Testament. This collection is commonly called the canon. We will consider the Christian attitude toward and use of the Old Testament. This will be followed by a consideration of the development of authority for the Christians. An effort will be made to see what Christian writings were used and were considered authoritative during the late first century and on into the fourth century, when we can speak of the New Testament canon as being firmly fixed. This survey will conclude with a brief consideration of the history of each of the books now included in our New Testament. We shall come to the conclusion that God was much involved in the selection and preservation of his Word. We will see that the early Christians made wise choices in the books which were included in the canon, in contrast to those which were excluded.

English Translations of the New Testament

The final area of consideration will be a concise look at English translations of the New Testament. Most of us are dependent upon such translations for our understanding of God's revelation. How have they come about? Why do they differ? Can we have confidence in all of them? This survey will be quite brief, because there are good books available on this subject for those who wish to investigate the matter further. In this study, we shall discover that the King James Version was neither the first nor the last Authorized Version. We shall see that much of the common wording of our New Testament actually goes back to the work of William Tyndale. And we shall see that the real question is not what translation one uses, but whether one *believes* and *practices* what he reads in the New Testament. This is always the ultimate question, for the true gospel can be found in any of the translations.

Many questions will be raised in the process of this work. But they are always asked—and answered—with the desire that our confidence in the New Testament will be increased. No attempt will be made to challenge anything to be found in the New Testament. Rather, the goal is that when we are finished, we may acclaim: "This was God's message to his people in the first century. It is still his message to us today. And we are certain that no discoveries or work in the future will change the basic truth contained in God's Word."

1

Materials for Textual Study

Books come in all sizes, and except for some children's books, they have one thing in common—they are all printed on paper. Of course, not all paper is of the same quality and thickness. If one were to compare a book printed recently with one printed a century ago, the differences would be clear. The old books have pages that are thick and stiff. Today's book is made of paper that is thin and quite flexible. But both have pages of paper. The same would not be true of materials used in the ancient world, since paper was a much later development. The writing would not have been done by a printing press, but was printed by hand. Furthermore, in the earliest days, the materials were not in book form at all. They were on scrolls or rolls. The book form which we know so well was developed in the Christian era and may have been a Christian invention. Some have even suggested that Mark wrote the original text of his Gospel in book form. Such a book is known as a codex.

Materials Used in Writing

As we consider Christian writings, we discover that the earliest writing material was papyrus, which for several centuries was the chief material used in writing. The name reminds us of our word *paper,* and it was the paper of the time. However, it was neither as plentiful nor as cheap as paper. It was made by hand from the papyrus plant which grew in abundance in the Nile Delta of Egypt, as well as in a few other places. This plant grew to a height of twelve to fifteen feet, and its diameter might be as large as a man's wrist. The stem was cut into sections about one foot in length and then into thin strips. These strips were placed on a flat surface, parallel to one another. Then another layer was placed on top of these, but running up and down instead of across. These two layers were pressed together until they had become bonded to each other. This made a sheet of papyrus suitable for writing. Sheets were glued together to form a scroll, which might reach a length of as much as thirty-five feet, about as large a roll as could be handled with any ease. Such a roll could have contained a work the size of the Gospel of Luke or the Book of Acts.

It was relatively easy to write on papyrus, at least on the front side, following the strips of papyrus. The back side was rougher, mainly because the strips of papyrus were vertical rather than horizontal. In a scroll, only one side was normally used for writing, which was done in narrow columns to make it easy to read as one end was unrolled and the other end rolled up. These narrow columns carried over into the later book form in which three or four columns appear on a page. In a sense we have carried over this idea into modern times with Bibles printed two columns to a page.

However, papyrus was not durable and would soon perish in a damp climate. Only in an extremely dry climate, such as that of much of Egypt, could these papyrus documents be preserved. In the ancient world, they must have been common throughout all the Mediterranean area.

With the passage of time, it was only natural that Christians would want a more durable material for their writings. As early as the fourth century, they began to use vellum or parchment, made from the skins of cattle, sheep, goats, or antelopes. This was a relatively thin material, especially that made from antelopes. In addition to providing a good writing surface on both sides, it had a lasting quality that far surpassed papyrus. Until the invention of the printing press it remained the most common writing material. Parchment was quite expensive, however, and sometimes the original writing was erased and the parchment used a second time. Such a manuscript is called a palimpsest.

Writing was ordinarily done with a reed pen (3 John 13). A reed stalk was dried and then sharpened on one end. The point was slit, resembling the point of an ink pen which was common a generation ago. This type of pen was ideal for writing on papyrus. With the beginning of the use of parchment, quill pens came into use and became the most common instrument for writing.

Ink was commonly made out of soot, or lampblack, mixed with gum dissolved in water. This was a black ink. A reddish-brown ink was made from nutgalls. Later, red ink was sometimes used. Many manuscripts are enhanced with illustrations in beautiful color, although the ink tended to fade after a long period of time. Some manuscripts give indication that the letters were retraced at a later time.

The type of writing varied at different periods. Between the fourth and ninth centuries, most manuscripts were written with capital letters, called uncials. These were written without space between words, and there were very few punctuation marks, if any. No accents or breathing marks were used. There were just line after line of capital letters. The first verse of the Gospel of John would appear this way, using English words and letters in place of the Greek: INTHEBEGINNINGWASTHEWORDANDTHE-WORDWASWITHGODANDTHEWORDWASGOD. This made manuscripts difficult to read and copy and inevitably contributed to mistakes that the scribes made. Later manuscripts were written in minuscule (small) letters, sometimes called cursive style. This resembles today's handwriting. It was faster to write; there were spaces between words; accents and punctuation marks were used. The great majority of New Testament manuscripts used this style of writing.

It is difficult to classify New Testament manuscripts, since the standard classifications gloss over the descriptions of materials and style of writing. But the confusion is not as great as it seems on the surface. Greek manuscripts are usually divided into three groups: papyrus, uncial, and minuscule. Of course, the first describes the type of writing material. The other two are differentiated on the basis of the style of writing. Of these three categories, the uncial are usually considered to be the most important for the study of the New Testament text.

We must realize that the New Testament was originally written in Greek. While the native tongue of the original followers of Jesus was Aramaic, even those men probably also used Greek. As soon as the gospel spread beyond the confines of Palestine, it was in a Greek-speaking world, for Greek was the commonly spoken language of all the Roman Empire. Most people had a native language as well, but one could communicate in Greek almost anywhere. This made the task of the early missionary easier in terms of communication. Paul, who wrote almost half the books in the New Testament, was born in Cilicia, where the common language was Greek, although he suggests that his parents had retained the ancestral tongue (Phil. 3:5).

Papyrus Manuscripts

We begin our consideration of the New Testament manuscripts with the earliest written documents, although they are the latest additions to our witness to the text. These are the papyrus fragments. Older books dealing with the New Testament text make little or no reference to these writings. Writing in 1925, A. T. Robertson stated: "The papyri discoveries have not added much to our knowledge of the text of the New Testament."[1] Few of the papyri (plural of *papyrus*) were known until recent times. But now they have made a great contribution in both the study of the New Testament text and the study of the Greek language. Until the late nineteenth century, many thought New Testament Greek was a special language of the Holy Spirit, given for the specific purpose of recording the Bible. However, late in the nineteenth century, an ancient rubbish heap was uncovered at Oxyrhynchus, Egypt. Thousands of papyrus documents were discovered, and the language of these documents was quite similar to that found in our

New Testament. Thus, it was learned that the New Testament was written in the common Greek, the colloquial (spoken) Greek of the day. However, it was not until much later that substantial New Testament materials were found written on papyrus. At the present time, at least 88 papyri of portions of the New Testament have been found and studied. Many of these are quite small, but in recent years some larger manuscripts have been found.[2] Papyrus manuscripts are listed with a small letter p and a superimposed number, from p^1 to p^{88}. The following are the most important of the papyrus documents.

Three papyrus manuscripts make up the Chester Beatty collection. These were acquired by Sir Chester Beatty in 1930–31. The first of these is p^{45}, which now contains parts of thirty leaves from a codex which must have originally included about 110 leaves. This contained the text of all four of the Gospels plus the Book of Acts. Included in the surviving material are portions of thirteen leaves of Acts, two of Matthew, six of Mark, seven of Luke, and two of John. This codex was probably copied in the first half of the third century. It has the Gospels in what is known as the Western order: Matthew, John, Luke, and Mark.

The second of the Chester Beatty papyri is p^{46}, consisting of eighty-six leaves out of an original 104. It contains ten letters, all of which, at the time of copying, were considered to have been written by Paul. Hebrews follows immediately after Romans, but the Pastoral Epistles (1 Timothy, 2 Timothy, and Titus) are not included. Philemon is also missing from the manuscript. The letters seem to have been placed in the order of length, with Romans listed first and 2 Thessalonians last. Dated from the early part of the third century, p^{46} is perhaps as early as A.D. 200.

The third manuscript in this collection is p^{47}, containing ten leaves out of the Book of Revelation. This is about one-third of the book, with the opening and closing chapters missing. It contains Revelation 9:10 to 17:2, with some omissions, and is dated in the middle or the last part of the third century.

Another papyrus fragment of great significance is p^{52}, the John Rylands fragment. It was discovered by C. H. Roberts among some papyri acquired by B. P. Grenfell in 1920. This piece of papyrus measures only about 2½ by 3½ inches, so its importance does not come from its size. Deriving its value from its early date, it is usually considered to have been copied in the first half of the second century (about A.D. 125–135 are the most common dates suggested for it). It contains only a small portion of the Gospel of John (18:31–33, 37–38). This shows that the Gospel was circulating in Egypt in the first half of the second century. And it also indicates that the book form was already in use at this early date, for the fragment has writing on both sides. It is the earliest fragment of the New Testament that has been found.

About twenty-five years after the acquiring of the Chester Beatty collection, another collection of papyrus was amassed by Martin Bodmer. Two of the manuscripts in this collection are of the utmost importance for the study of the New Testament text. One, p66, originally contained all of the text of the Gospel of John. Much of the text of the opening thirteen chapters is still in the manuscript, while fragments of the remainder of the Gospel are also preserved. This manuscript can most likely be dated about A.D. 200.

The other extremely valuable manuscript in the Bodmer collection is p75. This manuscript contained all of the Gospels of Luke and John, most of which have been preserved, and is also extremely early, usually being dated between A.D. 175 and 225. It is by far the earliest manuscript we have of Luke and one of the earliest of John.

The other papyri date from the third to the eighth centuries. All of the New Testament books are represented except 1 Timothy and 2 Timothy, although some of the others are found only in the later papyri. For example, 2 John and 3 John are included only in p74, a seventh-century fragment.

Uncial Manuscripts

Those involved in the study of the New Testament text consider the uncial manuscripts the most important for the establishment of the original text. They are not only earlier than the minuscule manuscripts (see below, p. 30) in date, but they also represent all of the text types. As previously mentioned, uncial manuscripts are written in capital letters, usually with no spaces between words. They are copied on vellum or parchment. The latest figures state that there are 274 of these manuscripts of the Greek New Testament or portions of it. They are usually designated by a capital letter. J. J. Wettstein began assigning letters to uncial manuscripts in 1751–52, using the English alphabet. Later, Greek letters were used and, finally, the first letter of the Hebrew alphabet. Since it became obvious that there were not enough capital letters to list all of this type of manuscript, they are now also listed with a number beginning with 0. Codex B is also known as 03. Only the manuscripts of special interest will be mentioned in this writing.

It is generally agreed that the most valuable of all the manuscripts of the New Testament is B, Codex Vaticanus. This manuscript has been in the Vatican Library in Rome since before 1475. It is apparently listed in the first catalogue of that library which was made in that year. Scholars estimate that this manuscript was copied in the middle of the fourth century, about A.D. 350. Some have suggested that this was one of the fifty manuscripts which Emperor Constantine ordered prepared for the churches of Constantinople after he became a Christian. Whether or not this is so, it is recognized that the text of this manuscript is ancient and extremely valuable. It was probably copied in Egypt, perhaps in Alexandria, and originally contained the entire Bible, including most of the Apocrypha. However, with the passage of time, the opening chapters of Genesis have been lost, along with some of the Psalms. In addition, the concluding portion of the New Testament has been lost. All of Hebrews from 9:14 is missing, along with 1 Timothy, 2 Timothy, Titus, Philemon, and Revelation. For some reason, access to this manuscript was difficult until 1868.

When F. C. Tischendorf visited the Vatican Library in 1843 to see the manuscript, he was allowed only six hours to study it. Two years later, S. P. Tregelles was carefully searched on entering and leaving the Library to make certain that he did not copy anything from Vaticanus. However, by the end of the nineteenth century, photographic copies of the manuscript were available for all scholars to use. The manuscript is copied on vellum made from antelope skins. There are three narrow columns on each page, reminding one of the narrow columns that would be found on a scroll. From forty to forty-four lines are in each column, and each line has from sixteen to eighteen letters. Probably at least three scribes were involved in the copying of the manuscript, with one of them doing almost all of the work on the New Testament. A number of correctors later worked on the manuscript.

Second in importance to B is Aleph, Codex Sinaiticus. This manuscript also dates from the fourth century and is only a little later than B. It, too, may have been one of the Bibles ordered by Emperor Constantine. The story of the discovery of this manuscript is fascinating.

F. C. Tischendorf perhaps contributed more to the accumulation of materials for textual study than any other man. He made many extensive journeys during the nineteenth century to find, study, and publish New Testament manuscripts. In 1844, he visited the monastery of St. Catherine on the slopes of Mount Sinai. He happened to see a number of vellum leaves in a container where they had been placed to be used for kindling fires. On examining these obviously ancient leaves, he discovered that they were portions of the Septuagint (a Greek translation of the Old Testament). In fact, Tischendorf recognized them as the most ancient leaves he had ever seen. He managed to rescue forty-three leaves from the fire, only to be told that two baskets of similar leaves had already been burned.

The leaves Tischendorf found contained portions of 1 Chronicles, Jeremiah, Nehemiah, and Esther. However, his interest in these leaves caused the monks to hide the remainder of the manuscript. All his efforts to gain possession of it failed at this time. He was permitted to take these leaves with him when he left, and they were placed in the University Library in Leipzig, Germany. In 1859, Tischendorf made his third trip to the monastery. His efforts to find the ancient manuscript proved fruitless until the day before he was to leave. On that day, a steward revealed that he had an ancient copy of the Septuagint. He took Tischendorf to his cell and produced the remainder of the manuscript which Tischendorf had been seeking. He was given permission to take it to his room for the night and discovered it to be far more important than he had guessed. It contained not only much of the Old Testament but the entire New Testament, plus two early Christian writings, the Epistle of Barnabas and the Shepherd of Hermas. This is the only uncial manuscript containing the entire New Testament and has four narrow columns per page, with forty-eight lines in each column. While three scribes worked in copying the Bible, one of them copied most of the New Testament, probably in Egypt.

Tischendorf was convinced that this manuscript was the most valuable one in existence. By this time, all the letters of the English alphabet and part of the Greek alphabet had been used in the list of uncials. He could not accept the idea of giving it a letter far down the alphabet, so he started over again with the Hebrew alphabet! This is the reason we know it as Aleph. Fortunately, the other Hebrew letters were never used in designating manuscripts.

Tischendorf sought to buy the manuscript but without success, and he returned to Cairo without the great treasure. However, through the efforts of monks at a sister monastery in Cairo, the manuscript was sent to Cairo and he was given permission to see it, eight leaves at a time. He hired two men in Cairo to help him with the copying, and in two months they copied the entire manuscript—110,000 lines. Later the manuscript was given to the Czar of Russia (the monastery was Eastern Orthodox), and it was placed in the library at Leningrad. In 1933, it was sold to the British Museum for 100,000 pounds (then over $500,000). This may not be the end of the story. In May, 1978, newspaper reports referred to significant new finds in a wall of the monastery of St. Catherine. Included in these finds were some pages of the Old Testament from Codex Sinaiticus. Much of the Old Testament of this manuscript has not been found. However, up to this time, no confirmation of this story has been published.

A number of other uncial manuscripts are worthy of brief

notice. Codex Alexandrinus, A, was copied in the fifth century. It contains most of the Old Testament as well as most of the New Testament. A large part of the Gospel of Matthew is missing, as well as portions of John and 2 Corinthians. In 1627, A was given to King Charles I of England by Cyril Lucar, Patriarch of Constantinople. Thus, it arrived in England a few years too late to influence the King James Version of the Bible. This manuscript represents two of the textual families (see chapter 2 for a discussion of the four textual families). In the Gospels, it is the oldest representative of the Byzantine text, and thus is not considered very important by many. However, in the remainder of the New Testament, it represents the Alexandrian text and is one of the most valuable manuscripts.

Codex Ephraemi, C, is also a fifth-century manuscript. It is a palimpsest. The text was erased in the twelfth century and the leaves used to record sermons of St. Ephraem. A. T. Robertson commented: "It is not the only time that sermons have covered up the Bible, alas."[3] Tischendorf had been able to read part of the original text, and in more recent times, the use of chemical agents has enabled scholars to recover most of the text of this manuscript. While it is an old manuscript, its text is not as valuable as some others because it is copied from various textual types. Only a little more than one-half of the New Testament remains in this manuscript.

One of the most interesting of the ancient manuscripts is Codex Bezae, D. The dating of this manuscript is uncertain although most would place it from either the fifth or sixth century. It contains only the four Gospels and Acts, along with a brief part of 3 John. What makes this manuscript so interesting and valuable is that it is written in two languages, Greek and Latin. The two languages face each other on opposing pages. The Latin is on the right-hand page, the position of honor. The Latin does not appear to be a translation of the Greek but was copied from Old Latin manuscripts. The Gospels are in the order Matthew, John, Luke, and Mark, those attributed to apostles thus being given primary positioning. This manuscript is the major representative of the Western text in the Gospels and Acts. One of the most interesting features of the manuscript is the way in which it departs from the traditional text, especially in Luke and Acts. In Luke, there are a number of omissions, such as Peter's running to the tomb (24:12), and the reference to the cup as following the breaking of the bread in the institution of the Last Supper (Luke 22:19b–20). In Acts, there are many long additions to the text, making it about one-tenth longer than the traditional text. One of the unsolved puzzles of textual study is why this manuscript differs so drastically from the text found in other manuscripts. Many suggestions have been made, one of which is that Luke may have issued his writings in two editions, one of which is represented in D.

Closely related to codex D is Codex Claromontanus, D^p or D_2. This is also a representative of the Western text, with both Latin and Greek texts. A sixth-century manuscript containing Paul's letters, including Hebrews, it is a major witness in determining the original text of these letters.

Manuscript W, the Washington Codex, is the oldest uncial manuscript of the New Testament housed in any library in the United States. It was found in Egypt in 1906 by Charles L. Freer and is now in the Freer Museum in the Smithsonian Institute in Washington, D.C. This manuscript contains the Gospels and is dated from the fourth or fifth century. It represents all four textual types. All of Matthew and Luke 8:13–24:53 are Byzantine. Mark 1:1–5:30 is Western; 5:31–16:20 is Caesarean. Luke 1:1–8:12 and John 5:12–21:25 are Alexandrian. The rest of John was added to the manuscript at a later date and represents a mixed text. The scribe who copied this manuscript may have changed manuscripts at the points where the text type changes, or the text from which he copied may already have been composed of the mixture. The manuscript is also interesting because of the insertion which it makes at Mark 16:14.

> And they excused themselves, saying, 'This age of law-lessness and unbelief is under Satan, who does not allow the truth and power of God to prevail over the unclean things of the spirits. Therefore reveal thy righteousness now'—thus

they spoke to Christ. And Christ replied to them, 'The term of years for Satan's power has been fulfilled, but other terrible things draw near. And for those who have sinned I was delivered over to death, that they may return to the truth and sin no more; that they may inherit the spiritual and incorruptible glory of righteousness which is in heaven.'[4]

Codex Koridethi, Theta, is a rather late uncial, being dated from the eighth or ninth century. Although it contains only the Gospels, it is significant because it is the chief uncial representative of what is known as the Caesarean text.[5]

Minuscule Manuscripts

The most numerous manuscripts of the New Testament are the minuscules or cursives. Written in a running hand, much as we write today, they are characterized by spaces between words as well as by punctuation marks. There are at least 2,795 of these manuscripts. Most of them are late, after the ninth century, and represent the late, or Byzantine, text. Two groups of these manuscripts are of special interest. (It will be noted that minuscule manuscripts are designated by the use of Arabic numbers.)[6]

Family 1 (f^1), or the Lake group, was identified by Kirsopp Lake early in the twentieth century. The group consists of four manuscripts (1, 118, 131, and 209) with at least four other very closely related manuscripts (22, 1278, 1582, and 2193). These manuscripts all contain basically the same text and often agree with Codex Koridethi. Thus, they are representative of the Caesarean text. The manuscripts come from the twelfth to the fourteenth centuries.

Family 13 (f^{13}), the Ferrar group, was isolated by W. H. Ferrar in the nineteenth century. The family contains about twelve manuscripts from the eleventh to the fifteenth centuries. (The manuscripts included are 13, 69, 124, 230, 346, 543, 788, 826, 828, 983, 1689, and 1709.) These all come from a common ancestor. One indication of this is that all have the story of the woman taken in adultery (John 7:53–8:11) following Luke 21:38. These manuscripts are also closely related to the Caesarean text.

Lectionaries

A final group of Greek manuscripts are known as lectionaries. These are manuscripts which contain selected passages of Scripture which have been copied out for use in church services, much like the responsive readings in our hymnals. At least 2,207 of these have been catalogued. However, since relatively little study of them has been made up to the present time, they make little contribution to our study of the New Testament text.

Versions

At an early date, efforts were made to translate the New Testament into other languages. Such translations are known as versions. Of them, the most important for the study of the text of the New Testament are the Latin, Syriac, and Coptic. These were undoubtedly made by Christians for use in spreading the gospel into areas where Greek would not have been widely used. While they are of value in establishing certain aspects of the Greek text, they also have limitations. Since the Latin has no definite article, Latin manuscripts cannot help us in seeking to determine whether the original Greek had an article. Syriac cannot distinguish between certain of the tenses in Greek, such as the aorist and the perfect. The Coptic does not have a passive voice.[7] However, these versions can show whether a particular passage was present in the Greek manuscript from which the translation was made. Of course, the more literal the translation, the greater its value in textual study.

Perhaps the most important of the versions was the Latin. Probably the earliest translations into Latin were made in North Africa in the late second century. Later translations were made in Italy. These translations are referred to as the Old Latin. About thirty-two manuscripts of portions of the New Testament in the Old Latin are still in existence. These were copied between the fourth and thirteenth centuries and are divided into two groups, the African and the European. Of these, the African are generally the oldest. Old Latin manuscripts are designated by the use of a small letter (a, b).

The Old Latin manuscripts became so numerous and varied that, in the late fourth century, Jerome was commissioned by Pope Damasus to prepare a new Latin translation which would replace all of the existing versions. Evidently he did rather careful work on the Gospels, and it appears that he used an Old Latin text and compared it with Greek manuscripts available to him. But his work on the remainder of the New Testament was much more rapid and less thorough. This may have been because of the criticism that his work on the Gospels received. Many people did not like it because it differed from what was familiar to them. The translation by Jerome became the basis for the Latin Vulgate, of which more than 8,000 manuscripts exist. The Latin manuscripts are representative of the Western text.

A second ancient and valuable version is the Syriac. Again, more than one Syriac version exists. Two manuscripts of the Gospels exist which represent the Old Syriac version. These are the Curetonian, edited by William Cureton in 1858 (designated sy[c]), and the Sinaitic (sy[s]), discovered at St. Catherine's monastery in 1892 by Mrs. Agnes Smith Lewis. Of the two, the Sinaitic is probably slightly older. The manuscripts were copied in the fourth or fifth centuries, but represent texts which were in use about two hundred years earlier. These two manuscripts are Western in text.

By the beginning of the fifth century, the Peshitta Syriac (sy[p]), or common, version was prepared. Second Peter, 2 and 3 John, Jude, and Revelation were not included in this translation. These books were not translated into Syriac until the sixth century. In most places the Peshitta text is Byzantine. Other Syriac translations were made later, but they are not as valuable for determining the early Greek text.

The other important ancient version of the New Testament is the Coptic. This is a late form of the ancient Egyptian language, written in Greek characters. By the third century, Christian writings were being translated into this language, first in the Sahidic (sa), and then in the Bohairic (bo) dialect. Both of these represent the Alexandrian text with some Western readings.

Of course, the New Testament was translated into many other

languages in the early centuries. Although these are not so valuable for the study of the text, it is possible that some late version might retain an original reading not found in the Greek manuscripts.

Church Fathers

One final source of help in the study of the text is found in the writings of the early Christians, often referred to as the Church Fathers. Christian writings from as early as A.D. 95 have been preserved. Some of these have many citations of the New Testament Scriptures, while others have only a few. Some references seem to be exact quotations, but others are mere allusions. Of course, one can never be certain whether the writer was quoting from memory or was copying from a text. Unfortunately, we cannot be sure we have the exact text of the Fathers, since their original manuscripts have been lost. Textual criticism must be applied to the surviving manuscripts in an effort to discover the original form of their writings. Another problem in the use of the Fathers is that sometimes their quotations of Scripture have been changed in the process of copying to agree with the textual tradition current at the time of copying. Thus, the value derived from these sources is limited. They are of greatest help in localizing and dating readings and types of text and of special value when they make reference to the differences in manuscripts with which the writers were familiar. The earliest of the Fathers preserve the Western type of text.

Thus, we see that the student of the New Testament text has a great supply of resources for his or her study. In fact, it sometimes seems that the resources are too great, for it is extremely difficult to bring together all the witnesses to a reading. However, by proper use of the major sources, the uncial manuscripts and the papyri, and with the support of the other materials, the original text of the New Testament can be determined with a great deal of confidence and accuracy. The story of the development of this type of study is the next subject of consideration.

2

History of the Printed New Testament Text

In any consideration of the development of the New Testament text, the key event must be the invention of printing with movable type. This took place in the middle of the fifteenth century. Prior to that time, copies of documents had to be made by hand. The work was slow and laborious, and the copies were inexact and expensive. But all this changed with the development of the printing press. The first book printed with movable type, in 1456, was a copy of the Bible in Latin, the Vulgate. It was about fifty years before a copy of the Greek text was printed.

Prior to the invention of the printing press, little specific work was done to develop an accurate Greek text of the New Testament. Perhaps no one was interested in doing it, and the materials were not available even if someone had shown a desire. Two names do stand out during the period. Origen was head of the catechetical school (a school for new Christians) in Alexandria, Egypt, early in the third century. Later he moved to Caesarea and founded a school there. He was a capable scholar and seemed to have a real interest in interpreting Scripture. In the process of interpretation, he also commented on differences which he found in the manuscripts which were available to him. However, there is no evidence that he sought to develop or edit a text. His method of interpretation led him to select from the various readings the one which best served his purposes.

Another person of stature was Jerome. In the fourth century, because many Latin translations were in existence, he was commissioned to make a standard Latin version of the Bible. The many translations did not agree with one another and were thought to be confusing. This required some comparison of the Latin versions with Greek manuscripts. We know of no objective principles used in the selection of readings for Jerome's version. Beyond the work of these two men, anything else that we may say about these early centuries is conjectural. It is true that editions of the Septuagint (the Greek translation of the Old Testament) were prepared on at least two occasions. But there is no evidence that similar work was done on the text of the New Testament.

Earliest Printed Texts

By the early sixteenth century, the situation began to change. One reason for this was the possibility of making many copies of a book quickly and accurately. But another important factor was the revival of interest in the Greek language in Western Europe. Many people, some of good education, were driven from Asia Minor and Greece into Western Europe. They brought with them a new interest in learning and scholarship, as well as a knowledge of the Greek language. With the passage of time, interest in the Greek text of the New Testament revived, even though the Latin Vulgate retained its primary place.

The publication of the Greek text of the New Testament got off to something less than a rousing beginning. A Spanish cardinal, Francisco Ximenes de Cisneros, prepared a Bible in several languages. The Old Testament was in Hebrew, Greek, and Latin, with the Latin in the center column, and the New Testament was in Greek and Latin. This was known as the Complutensian Polyglot, named for the university town of Alcala (in Latin, Complutum) where it was printed. The New Testament volume was printed in 1514. It is not known which Greek manuscripts were used in the preparation of the text. In the dedication of the volume to Pope Leo X, mention is made of receiving manuscripts from the Vatican Library in Rome.[1] It is likely that most of the manuscripts were late. While one of the most ancient and best manuscripts of the Bible, Codex Vaticanus, was in the Vatican Library at that time, there is no indication that Ximenes had access to it.

Unfortunately, the text of the Complutensian Polyglot had little influence on the development of the New Testament text, although its text was probably better prepared than that of its early rival. One reason for this lack of influence is that Ximenes had to wait several years before he received permission from the pope to publish his work. It was 1522 before this permission was received, and by that time another edition was on the market. The New Testament text grew out of this rival work instead of that of Ximenes.

The first *published* Greek New Testament was edited by Erasmus, the leading scholar in Western Europe in the early sixteenth century. Evidently John Froben, a printer in Basle, Switzerland, learned what Ximenes was doing in Spain. He sensed that the time was ripe for the marketing of a Greek New Testament, and he sought to be the first on the market with such a volume. He enlisted Erasmus to produce this work, which was done in a period of about ten months. The process was so hasty that Erasmus himself later admitted that the work was "precipitated rather than edited."[2] It was filled with typographical errors. In addition, Erasmus was limited by the number and quality of Greek manuscripts available for use. For the most part, he seemed to depend most on two twelfth-century manuscripts. He had a few other manuscripts but did not make much use of the better ones because he was afraid of what seemed to be an erratic text in them. Erasmus had no Greek manuscript which contained the last six verses of the book of Revelation. To complete his text, he translated those verses into Greek from the Latin Vulgate. Thus, there are readings in his text that have never been found in any Greek manuscript. And some of these readings were carried over into what is known as the *Textus Receptus,* or Received Text. This edition by Erasmus was published in 1516 and became the basis for the Greek text for the next three centuries.

Erasmus issued new editions of his text in 1519, 1522, 1527, and 1535. The edition of 1522 was the most important. One of the criticisms made against his text was that he had omitted from 1 John 5:7–8 the words: ". . . in heaven, the Father, the Word, and the Holy Ghost: and these three are one. And there are three that bear witness in earth" (KJV). Stunica, one of those who had helped Ximenes in his edition, visited Erasmus to ask him why he had not included these words, which had appeared for many centuries in the Latin Vulgate. Erasmus replied that he had not found them in any Greek manuscript. He promised to put them in his next edition if he saw a Greek manuscript which contained them. Some months passed. Once more Erasmus had a visitor. This time he produced a scroll containing the Greek text of 1 John, and in this text were the words which Erasmus had omitted from his published text. Seemingly, this manuscript had been prepared for the special benefit of Erasmus. It was probably copied in Oxford about 1520 by a Franciscan named Roy, so it could be shown to Erasmus.[3] And Erasmus kept his promise by inserting the disputed words in his text of 1522, although he must have known what had been done. Thus, these words became part of the Received Text of the Greek New Testament for three hundred years, and they made their way into the King James Version of 1611.

Erasmus' text of 1519 was the material used by Martin Luther for his German translation of the New Testament. Erasmus made many changes in the edition of 1527, based to a large extent on having seen a copy of Ximenes' work. However, these changes did not get into the textual tradition, because his edition of 1522 was the one used by his successors.

Development of the Received Text

The next person of importance in the history of the text is Robert Estienne, better known as Stephanus, who issued four editions of the Greek New Testament (1546, 1549, 1550, and 1551). He had a few more manuscripts than did Erasmus, about fourteen in number. These included Codex Bezae, an early and important witness to the text of the Gospels and Acts, and Stephanus used these to correct Erasmus' edition of 1522. His edition of 1550 was the first to contain variant readings.[4] On the inner margin, Stephanus listed readings from the various manuscripts, where they differed from his text. This edition became the Received Text for England, and thus served as the basis for the translation of the King James Version of the New Testament. Stephanus' edition of 1551 was the first to contain verse divisions (chapter divisions had been in use since about 1228). This work was done on a trip between Paris and Lyons. A. T. Robertson commented: "I have often felt that the horse sometimes bumped his pen into the wrong place."[5] By this, he was indicating that the verse divisions sometimes seem to be made at a most inappropriate place. However, it is likely that the work was done in the inns where Stephanus stopped to spend the nights on his journey.

Theodore Beza, the successor of John Calvin in Geneva, Switzerland, published nine editions of the New Testament between 1565 and 1604. He made much use of the work of Stephanus, and his editions tended to fix that text as the established one. It was through Beza's work that the text of Stephanus became the fixed text for England and served as the basis for the translation of the King James Version.

The final people of importance in this earliest period are two German printers, Bonaventure and Abraham Elzevir. They published seven editions of the Greek New Testament between 1624 and 1678, and their text seems to have been based mainly on that of Stephanus. In the preface to their edition of 1633, they inserted this claim: "[the reader has] the text which is now received by all, in which we give nothing changed or corrupted."[6] Little did they know how influential this statement would become, although it was actually little more than a publisher's advertisement. There was no justification for the claim, as this was not the text that was accepted by all. Although it was far from being without change or corruption, people soon came to believe the claim was true. It was from this statement that the term "Received Text," or *Textus Receptus,* was derived, and, on the basis of this claim, it did become the text which was accepted for two hundred years. During this period, it was almost impossible to change the text. No printer would have printed a different text and, even if he had, no one would have purchased it. Thus we come to the period when the Received Text reigned supreme.

Supremacy of the Received Text

The period of the reign of the Received Text was from 1633 to 1831—a time when no really new text of the New Testament could be printed. However, it was far from being an unimportant time, since many things were taking place which were preparing the way for the development of a better text of the New Testament. More manuscripts were becoming available, variant readings were being collected, and gradually a theory of textual study was being developed. Although all of this took the time and skill of many people, only the most significant developments can be mentioned.

John Mill of Oxford published an important edition of the Greek New Testament in 1707, and sought to collect evidence from Greek manuscripts, early versions, and the Church Fathers. He made use of almost eighty Greek manuscripts in his edition. Although it is true that Mill reprinted Stephanus's text of 1550, he listed about 30,000 variants from this text. In his discussions of the text, he made reference to almost one-half of the verses in the New Testament. This was a monumental work, as it put forth in clear form the fact that the text of the New Testament could not be affirmed to be a fixed thing. The reality of so many variants in the manuscripts was a matter which would require the attention and best efforts of generations of the finest scholars. While Mill's work was of more lasting importance, it should be noted that the first man to seek to desert the Received Text and publish a complete New Testament, giving more ancient readings, was Edward Wells (1709–1719). He departed from the Elzevir text in 210 places.[7]

Richard Bentley is the next person of importance in the history of the text, although he did not publish an edition of the New Testament. In 1720, he published *Proposals for Printing*, a six-page summary of what he hoped to do with the New Testament text. He printed the last chapter of Revelation as an example of the type of work he thought he could do. This Cambridge scholar had for some years been interested in textual study. His desire was to restore the New Testament text of the fourth century. He believed that, by using the oldest Greek manuscripts and the oldest manuscripts of Jerome's Vulgate, he could establish this text so that no one could question its accuracy. He raised a considerable sum of money toward the carrying out of this project, but it never went any further.[8]

Of course, the text of the fourth century was not the proper goal. While it would have been superior to the texts then available, it would not have been the original text of the New Testament. Perhaps one of the assumptions of the time was that little or no change in the text took place in the early centuries. Today we know this to be a false assumption. In fact, it is likely that almost all the important changes in the text took place within the first one hundred years after the writing of the New Testament books.

> The variants which require consideration in textual criticism, however, arose for the most part in the earliest period of textual history. This period of *divergence of manuscripts* may be said to extend to the time when Christianity had established itself as the religion of the Roman Empire, although even the first half of this period likely saw the introduction of most of the variants.[9]

One of the most important names in eighteenth-century study of the New Testament is that of Johann Albrecht Bengel (1687–1752), who issued his edition of the New Testament in 1734. He has been called the father of modern textual criticism.[10] With him, the center of study of the text moved from England to the European continent. The next English scholar of note in textual study does not appear for another century. While it is true that the text published by Bengel did not depart significantly from the Received Text, yet he set forth certain principles that were to influence the history of textual study from that time forward.

As a student, Bengel had been disturbed by the long list of

variants published by Mill. He feared this brought into question the inspiration of Scripture. After careful study of all the materials available, he came to the conclusion that the variants were fewer than might have been expected and that they did not call into question any evangelical doctrine.

Bengel's work is important in three areas. He was the first to divide manuscripts into groups which can be called families. He pinpointed two of these groups: the Asiatic and the African. The Asiatic came from Constantinople and included the manuscripts copied at a later time. The African was represented by the older manuscripts and included Codex Alexandrinus (a fifth-century manuscript) and the Old Latin. This grouping of manuscripts into families led to the conclusion that, in studying a reading, manuscripts must be weighed—not counted. By this, Bengel meant that it was not important *how many* manuscripts supported differing readings. What was important was what the manuscripts were and their relative value, or what family they represented. This principle took undue weight away from the later, much more numerous, and more inaccurate manuscripts.

A second area in which Bengel made a contribution was in the formulation of a principle of criticism which has been generally accepted since his time. He insisted that the more difficult reading is to be preferred to the easier reading. This was because a scribe was more likely to change a difficult construction into one which was easier, at least from his perspective.

The final contribution of Bengel was in the classification of variant readings. Prior to his time, these readings were simply listed, with no attempt made to evaluate them. Bengel divided them into five categories. One group consisted of those he considered to be the original text (yet he did not feel that he could put them into his printed text). The second group included those which were better than the printed text, the third were the readings which were as good as the printed text. A fourth category included the readings which were inferior to the text. And the final group denoted the readings which were to be rejected. The contributions of Bengel could not be ignored, although they were bitterly opposed by some.

The next important figure was John Jakob Wettstein (1693–1754), who had worked with Bengel in his early years. His efforts were misunderstood and resulted in his being driven from the church which he pastored. Wettstein became a professor in Amsterdam and published an edition of the New Testament in 1751–52. Unfortunately, he had come to the conclusion that all of the early Greek manuscripts had been contaminated by the Latin.[11] Later editors had to overcome this idea before progress could be made. Wettstein was the first to designate uncial manuscripts by capital letters and minuscule manuscripts by Arabic numbers.

Johann Salomo Semler (1725–91) expanded the work of Bengel on families. He incorrectly applied the term *recension* to these ancient texts. Actually the term means "a work of criticism by editors,"[12] but Semler seemed to use it simply to refer to families. In place of Bengel's two families, he believed there were three: the Alexandrian, which came from Origen and included such versions as the Syriac and Ethiopic; the Oriental or Eastern, which was used at Antioch and Constantinople; and the Western, found in the Latin version and the Church Fathers.

The beginning of the critical text of the New Testament is credited to Johann Jakob Griesbach (1745–1812), who devoted much time to the collation of manuscripts. To collate a manuscript means to compare it against a standard text and note every point at which it differs from the standard. This is a laborious but necessary task in developing an accurate text. Griesbach gave much attention to the quotations of the New Testament in the Fathers, who wrote in Greek, and to some of the little-studied versions. But it was in the area of the transmission of the text that he made his greatest contributions. "The task which lay before Griesbach was to vindicate the authority of the older codices, to classify authorities, and to use them critically and consistently for the restoration of the text."[13] He, like Semler, thought of three textual families: Alexandrian, Western, and Byzantine. His groups are generally supported by modern editors, even though the number of manuscripts today is much larger than was available to Griesbach.

For the first time, a German scholar was able to print a text of the New Testament (1775–77) which at some points departed significantly from the Received Text. But an equally important contribution was the development of a "theory of textual criticism that compelled attention."[14] He set forth several canons (principles) of criticism. Briefly stated, these include: no reading is preferred unless it is supported by ancient manuscripts; all criticism of the text depends upon classes of documents; the shorter reading is preferred to the longer; the more difficult reading is preferred to the easier; and the reading which appears false at first is preferred.[15]

Development of a Critical Text

The undisputed reign of the Received Text began to break down in 1831 with the work of Carl Lachmann (1793–1851). Perhaps the fact that he was not a theologian assisted him in making the break with the Received Text. He was a professor of classical philology in Berlin. As such, he had studied the texts of many of the ancient Greek writers and had published editions of their writings. He believed that the same principles could be used to establish the text of the New Testament. In 1831, Lachmann published a Greek New Testament based on purely documentary evidence. He made no claims that he was publishing the original text of the New Testament, since he thought this was impossible. He merely attempted to publish the text of the fourth century. He used only some of the early uncials, the Old Latin, the Vulgate of Jerome, and the witness of Irenaeus, Origen, and a few of the other Fathers. His sources were not adequate to complete what he attempted in a successful manner. Unfortunately, Lachmann failed to include any discussion of his methods in the volume in which he published his text. Rather, he referred his readers to an article he had published a year earlier in a German periodical in which such information was set forth. While he was strongly opposed by many and misunderstood by others, his work has received high praise in attaining a new point of development of the New Testament text. F. J. A. Hort said of his work:

> A new period began in 1831, when for the first time a text was constructed directly from the ancient documents without the intervention of any printed edition, and when the first systematic attempt was made to substitute scientific method for arbitrary choice in the discrimination of various readings. In both respects the editor, Lachmann, rejoiced to declare that he was carrying out the principles and unfulfilled intentions of Bentley, as set forth in 1716 and 1720.[16]

Perhaps the man who made the greatest contribution to modern textual study was Lobegott Friedrich Constantin von Tischendorf (1815–74). We have already told the story of his discovery of Codex Sinaiticus at St. Catherine's monastery. But that is only one small part of a long career dedicated to the finding and study of New Testament manuscripts. Appointed professor of theology at Leipzig, he made many journeys to collect and examine manuscripts. He is noted for his exact collation of more than twenty manuscripts. In addition, he published the exact text of about twenty-one manuscripts, so that they were available to a wider range of scholars. He also published eight editions of the Greek New Testament. While his skill in other areas is unquestioned, it seems that, as a critical editor, Tischendorf was less than what one could wish. In a sense, he was overimpressed by the latest manuscript which he had studied. For example, between the seventh and eighth editions, he made some 3,572 changes in text based primarily on the witness of Codex Sinaiticus, which he had discovered and studied since publication of the seventh edition.

Nevertheless, Tischendorf's eighth edition is still an indispensable tool for anyone who wishes to make a thorough study of the text. Not only does he give a text based on the reading of ancient manuscripts, but he also gives a massive critical apparatus[17] which lists all the varied readings which were known to his day from the manuscripts, versions, and Fathers. Unfortunately for most modern readers, this work is entirely in Greek and Latin. This edition was published between 1869 and 1872. Caspar René Gregory wrote an introduction (Prolegomena) to it in a third volume, published between 1884 and 1894.

While efforts have been under way for a number of years to bring the apparatus of Tischendorf up to date, there is still nothing that takes the place of his work. The mass of materials with which to work has grown so greatly that even with the use of the most modern methods it is almost impossible to assemble all the evidence in a workable form. We can be grateful for a man such as Tischendorf, who dedicated his entire life to the task of recovering the original text of the New Testament.

Study of the text once again returned to England in the work of Samuel P. Tregelles (1813–75). He published only one edition (1857–72), but it was based upon a careful study of the ancient manuscripts and used critical principles greatly similar to those developed by Lachmann. Tregelles was influential in helping to open the eyes of those in England to the need for a text other than the Received Text. Along with Tischendorf, he is considered the leading influence preparing the way for the development of the modern critical text. ". . . their indefatigable labours in the discovery and exhibition of fresh evidence, aided by similar researches on the part of others, provide all who come after them with invaluable resources not available half a century ago."[18]

But it was the work of two men, Brooke Foss Westcott (1825–1901) and Fenton John Anthony Hort (1828–92), that brought the critical text of the New Testament to a place of acceptance in the English-speaking world. By "critical text," one means a text based upon scientific principles and careful, detailed study. In many ways, their text, published in 1881, is the most important one that has been produced. They published their work in two volumes. Volume 1 contained the Greek text of the New Testament; and Volume 2 contained an introduction and appendix, giving the principles that the two men used in formulating their text and also discussing certain problem passages. This text served as the basis for the English Revised Version of 1881 and the later American Standard Version of 1901.

The great value of the work of these men came from their careful development of principles of criticism and the detailed application of these principles to the text. They divided evidence into two categories: external and internal. External evidence refers to the readings reflected in the extant Greek manuscripts of the New Testament, the versions, and the Fathers. Internal evidence is the consideration of the type of errors that scribes commonly made. On the basis of this consideration, Westcott and Hort came to the conclusion that manuscripts could be separated into families on the basis of ancestry. This, of course, was a further development of the work which Bengel had begun. They concluded that four families of manuscripts exist. Of these, the oldest and purest was given the name Neutral. They believed that it most frequently represented the true and original text, although even this family was not infallible. This text was best represented by Codex Sinaiticus and B (Vaticanus). A second text was the Alexandrian, which they believed was developed by a conscious correction of form and that it was polished in some Greek center such as Alexandria. This family was represented by manuscripts C and L, the Coptic versions, and some of the early Fathers—although no manuscript was a pure representative of the Alexandrian family. All such manuscripts contained readings from the other families. The third text was given the name of Western. This was represented by Codex Bezae (D) in the Gospels and Acts, D_2 (Codex Claromontanus) in the Epistles, by the Old Latin versions, and the Curetonian Syriac. This text, although old, had many strange variations and could not be trusted when it departed from the Neutral except in a few places where it omitted material. The final textual family was called the Syrian. This represented the latest revisions in the fourth century, designed to produce a smooth and complete text. It is represented by the late uncials and the vast proportion of the minuscule manuscripts and is the basis for the Received Text which dominated the field of textual study for over two centuries.

The edition of Westcott and Hort has served as the basis for most of the work on the Greek New Testament during the past century. It is true that it raised an outcry among some who were alarmed that they had given up the Received Text which was the basis of the King James Version. However, their ideas gradually carried the field and were accepted, at least in principle. This does not mean that no developments have taken place since their time. However, it is difficult to select men who have dominated the field since the days of Westcott and Hort.

During the current century, the most ambitious effort to develop a text of the New Testament and a new theory of criticism must be credited to Hermann von Soden (1852–1914). He developed a new method of designating manuscripts, a new theory of manuscript relationships, and a new text of the New Testament. It is a complex system and has never been accepted by most modern scholars and editors, although some of von Soden's ideas have been influential in the work of students of the discipline.

Today, two editions of the Greek New Testament are most regularly used. Both are, in some respects, closely related to the text of Westcott and Hort. The oldest of these is the text edited first by Eberhard Nestle (1851–1913) and later by his son, Erwin Nestle. It is now edited by Kurt Aland. The twenty-sixth edition of this text was published in 1979 in cooperation with the Education Committee which prepared the *Greek New Testament*, published by the United Bible Societies: Kurt Aland, Matthew Black, Carlo Martini, Bruce Metzger, and Allen Wikgren. The third edition of the United Bible Societies' text was published in 1975 under the sponsorship of the American Bible Society, British and Foreign Bible Society, National Bible Society of Scotland, Netherlands Bible Society, and Wurttemburg Bible Society. The five men listed above served as the Editorial Committee and the work was prepared in cooperation with the Institute for New Testament Textual Research at Münster, West Germany. The wording of these two editions is identical, although there are variations in punctuation, paragraphing, and textual apparatus.

Both of these texts serve as valuable and reliable editions which present the best results of centuries of scholarship in seeking to attain as closely as possible the original text of the New Testament. The methods by which this has been achieved will be considered in a subsequent chapter. Before that can be done, some attention must be given to the scribal practices in early centuries.

3

Scribal Practice

To understand how variations have multiplied in manuscripts, we must take a brief look at how documents were once copied. We have already mentioned the types of materials that were used. In the earliest years, papyrus was the chief writing material and in later times, parchment or vellum. Because vellum is more durable, it is only natural that most existing manuscripts are on vellum. Since each copy was handwritten, none was an exact duplicate of the manuscript from which it was copied. With each succeeding copy, the number of variations increased, since not only were previous errors continued, but new errors were introduced into each succeeding copy.

Use of Scribes in Writing

We are not certain how the original copies of our New Testament writings were produced, although it is almost certain they were written on papyrus. It appears that Paul was in the habit of dictating his letters to a scribe or secretary. We assume that, in most instances, he dictated word for word. However, it is possible that on occasion he might have expressed to a trusted friend the general idea which he wanted written. The friend would then have put Paul's ideas into his own words.

Some of the later manuscripts have subscriptions—notations at the end—that state the name of the secretary and even the place from which the letter was written. It is not known whether these merely represent old traditions or are the opinion of some scribe, based upon his knowledge of Paul's activities and perhaps gained from the Book of Acts. In either case, it is not likely that we can have much confidence in any of these notations.

However, there are indications in some of Paul's letters that he did indeed dictate the letters. In Romans 16:22, we find these words: "I Tertius, the writer of this letter, greet you in the Lord" (RSV). This does not mean that Tertius was the author of the letter. Rather, it seems that he was the one to whom Paul dictated the letter, and at this point he added his greetings to those of Paul. It is generally believed that Paul took the pen into his own hands at Galatians 6:11 and wrote the remainder of the letter himself. It is, of course, possible that he had written the entire letter himself, but it is not likely. Here, the reference to "large letters" has been understood to refer either to Paul's inexperience in writing or to his bad eyesight. Whatever it may mean, it suggests that in the original copy Paul's handwriting would have been quite distinct from that of the scribe who copied the remainder of the letter. Unfortunately, this difference would not be reproduced in later copies. Copy machines to produce exact replicas were not then available.

In the same way, Paul wrote: "I, Paul, write this greeting with my own hand. This is the mark in every letter of mine; it is the way I write" (2 Thess. 3:17, RSV). Earlier in this letter, the suggestion was made that a letter falsely attributed to Paul might be in circulation. Perhaps he added the closing greeting regularly to guarantee authenticity, much as one signs a letter today to give the same assurance.

We do not know if a similar practice was followed by other writers of New Testament letters, but it is quite likely. In fact, this has been one of the ways in which similarities between New Testament writings have been explained. Silvanus (Silas) was the scribe used in 1 Peter. This letter has close relationships with some of Paul's writings, and Silas was a companion of Paul in his travels. Perhaps Peter gave Silas a great deal of freedom in the composing of this letter. While there is no specific evidence, it is probable that the writers of the Gospels and Acts worked in the same way in the production of their writings.

Making of Copies

At a very early time, copies were made of these various writings. In the case of Paul's letters to the churches, perhaps some visitor from another city would be present when the letter was read in the services. He would be impressed by the letter and desire a copy to take home to his own church. If Ephesians was a circular letter written to a number of churches, it is possible that a copy would be made and left in each of these churches. The same thing might be true for the Book of Revelation, which has letters to seven churches in chapters 2 and 3. While the Gospels were perhaps originally produced for one church or one group of churches, it was inevitable that their value would be recognized as so great that copies would be desired for neighboring churches.

We are accustomed to thinking of publishing work as being done in large modern facilities—where type is set by experts, and proofreaders are employed to make certain that errors do not occur in the production of the text. Each book printed is identical with all the others printed at the same time. Even with these safeguards, however, we know that almost every book published has some sort of mistake in it. Not only were ancient methods not as advanced as ours, but the earliest copies of the New Testament were not made by professional scribes. In fact, it is likely that copies had to be made almost in secret for many years because of the attitude of the government toward Christianity. By the end of the first century, Christianity was at best suspect, and in some places it was the object of active persecution. In later years, Christians were compelled to surrender their writings to the authorities. It was not until the fourth century that Christians could use "publishing houses" for the production of their Scriptures.

Another important factor is that, when the earliest copies of New Testament writings were made, these writings were not looked upon as Scripture. It was at least a century after their writing before they were considered on this level. Thus there was not as much care taken in the copying as one could have wished. It was nothing as precise as the Jewish practice of copying their Scriptures. Jewish scribes would even count the individual characters in each line to make certain that nothing was left out or added. Furthermore, once the copy was determined to be accurate, the original would be destroyed, since these writings were looked upon as sacred and could not be allowed to remain in imperfect condition. Something of the freedom with which early Christian writings were treated may be seen in the way in which the authors of the Gospels of Matthew and Luke made use of Mark. (It is likely that Mark was the first Gospel to be written. Matthew and Luke used Mark in their writing.) They felt free to make many changes in arrangement and wording. Evidently, later scribes felt there were few restrictions in the way in which they changed the texts of manuscripts. It appears they sometimes deliberately changed the text from that which appeared before them. When a scribe took freedom in copying a manuscript, he complicated the task of getting back to what was originally written.

It is difficult for us to realize what toil was involved in the copying of manuscripts in the ancient world. We are accustomed to writing on smooth paper in comfortable surroundings with good lighting. None of these conditions was possible in the ancient world. Evidence from that period indicates that scribes did not sit at desks to write. They stood, or they sat on a stool or bench and held the scroll on their knees. Such a posture would not contribute to concentration.[1]

Scribes sometimes added notes at the end of their writing to indicate the difficult circumstances in which they worked. "He who does not know how to write supposes it to be no labour; but though only three fingers write, the whole body labours." "Writing bows one's back, thrusts the ribs into one's stomach, and fosters a general debility of the body." "As travellers rejoice to see their home country, so also is the end of a book to those who toil [in writing]." "The end of the book; thanks be to God!" And in one manuscript, the scribe noted that a heavy snow was falling outside, his ink froze, and his hand became numb and the pen fell from his fingers.[2] Of course, in the early years, those who copied New Testament manuscripts were Christians. They undoubtedly sensed a dedication to the task which helped overcome some of the discomfort they felt. However, we should remember the difficulty involved in the copying of a manuscript.

It was difficult for a scribe to avoid making mistakes when he copied a manuscript, even as it is difficult for us today. Anyone who has read papers where quotations are included will realize that errors of copying occur, even with the typewriter and careful reading. Add to the natural difficulties the fact that early copies of the Scriptures were written in capital letters with no space between words and no punctuation marks, and you begin to see how much more difficult it must have been to copy accurately. In addition, sometimes the materials on which the writing was placed were not free from blemishes. This could lead to confusing letters and even words. Sometimes the scribe was faced with decisions, since there might be material in the margin of the manuscript or between the regular lines. The scribe had to decide whether this was simply a marginal note or a correction that had been made and needed to be copied in the text of the manuscript. Even beyond this, it might be that a second manuscript would be used to make corrections as the copying was being done. When the two manuscripts disagreed, the scribe had to decide which one to follow.

Four operations were involved when a scribe was copying a manuscript. In each line or phrase he was copying, he had to read the words to himself or aloud. Then he needed to retain this material in his memory. This line or phrase then had to be dictated to himself silently or aloud. Finally, his hand had to move to copy what he had just dictated.[3]

After Christianity was made the official religion of the Roman Empire in the fourth century, it was possible for Christians to use professional publishing houses for the copying of their Scriptures. In such places, copying was done by a group of scribes, usually slaves. There might be as many as fifty of these seated or standing in the room. They would write while another slave read from a manuscript. Of course, this introduced new possibilities of error. The reader might not speak the words clearly, or the copyist might not hear distinctly what had been read. The fact that certain letters were pronounced alike led to the possibility of spelling errors. In addition, since these scribes might not be Christians, this could lead to carelessness in their work. And the work was expensive. It has been estimated that the cost of producing a Bible might have been forty times as great as the yearly salary of a Roman soldier.[4]

Yet, with all these difficulties, copies were made of the Scriptures. Many of the copies have been preserved for us, but probably many times more perished. Included among those which perished were the autograph copies. No one thought that they had special value. They would have been much used, and undoubtedly they quickly wore out, since papyrus does not have a long life when used regularly. When they became too worn, they would have been destroyed. Or they may have perished in the midst of persecution. There is no reason to suppose that copies of any of them will ever be discovered. We can be grateful to the many Christians in the early years who spent long hours copying these materials. In later centuries, the monks in the monasteries considered the copying of Scripture as one of their important tasks.

Scribal Errors

Having noted the ways in which scribes worked, it will now be helpful to see the kinds of errors to which they were susceptible. Errors are usually divided into two types, unintentional and intentional. We will give attention to the unintentional errors first. These can be considered in various ways, but most writers suggest they are related to the eye, ear, memory, and judgment.

Errors of the eye were frequent. Sometimes the scribe could not tell where one word was supposed to end and another begin (we must remember that in the uncial manuscripts there was no space between words). In 1 Timothy 3:16 are the Greek letters *homologoumenōs*. This could be either one word or two. If the letters make only one word, it should be translated "confessedly." If the letters form two words, the translation would be "we confess." Either makes sense in the context, and the uncial manuscripts are of no help in deciding which was the original form. Fortunately, this type of problem is rare in the New Testament.

Another error of the eye was the misunderstanding of, or the failure to recognize, the presence of abbreviations. It was common for scribes to abbreviate certain words related to deity, as well as other commonly used nouns. Among these were the words for God, Jesus, Christ, Son, Lord, and Spirit. An example of such confusion is again found in 1 Timothy 3:16. Does the quotation (probably of an early Christian hymn) begin with the word *God,* or the word *Who?* The word for "God," *theos,* would have been abbreviated *ths,* with a mark over the letters to indicate an abbreviation, while the word for "who" is *os.* The capital letters *theta* (th) and *omicron* (o) are very similar in appearance. It would have been easy for a scribe to see one but mistake it for the other. Another example occurs in 1 Corinthians 12:13. While most manuscripts read, "were made to drink one Spirit," others state, "were made to drink one drink." The difference is between *pma,* the abbreviation for *pneuma,* "Spirit," and *poma,* the word for "drink."

A number of Greek letters, especially capital letters, looked somewhat alike. Thus, it was easy to confuse *sigma* (s), *epsilon* (e), *theta* (th), and *omicron* (o). In the same way, *tau* (t), *pi* (p), and *gamma* (g) might be confused, especially if they were written hurriedly or carelessly. Thus, in 2 Peter 2:13, some manuscripts read *agapais* (love feasts) while others read *apatais* (deceptions). Here two confusions took place. *Gamma* (g) and *pi* (p) were confused, and then *pi* (p) and *tau* (t). Two *lambdas* (l) written closely together could look like *mu* (m). Thus, in Romans 6:5, some manuscripts read *alla* while others read *ama.* The difference in meaning between the words is that one means "but" and the other means "together." *Lambda* (l) and *iota* (i) written closely together could sometimes look like *nu* (n). Thus, in 2 Peter 2:18, there is the variation between *oligōs* (scarcely) and *ontōs* (really). In addition, *delta* (d) and *lambda* (l) could easily be confused.

Sometimes a scribe was confused when two lines, or even two

clauses, began or ended with the same words or letters. Thus, 1 John 2:23 reads: "No one who denies the Son has the Father. He who confesses the Son has the Father also" (RSV). Some manuscripts omit the words, "He who confesses the Son has the Father also." This may be because the first clause ends with the words "has the Father" (*ton patera echei*), and the second clause ends with the same words. It appears that the scribe copied the first "has the Father." When he looked back to read more of the text from which he was copying, he accidentally saw only the second occurrence of the words. Thus, he omitted everything between the two phrases. The same thing seems to have happened in John 6:39 where two manuscripts, including Sinaiticus, omit the first part of the verse, "This is the will of him who sent me." The last words of the previous verse are identical with the last words of the opening clause of verse 39. Once more, the eye of the scribe may have skipped from one clause to the other and omitted all the material in between. Many other examples of the same type of error can be found, ranging all the way from a few words to the omission of an entire verse (Luke 14:27; 18:39).[5]

It is only natural that the process can work in the opposite way. One may repeat the same word or phrase.[6] Perhaps the clearest example of this is found in Acts 19:34 where the cry of the crowd, "Great is Artemis of the Ephesians," is repeated in one manuscript, Vaticanus.

Sometimes errors were caused by the faulty hearing of the scribe. This happened when the manuscripts were copied from the reading by another person. One of the problems was that many of the vowels in Greek had a similar sound. The vowels *ēta* (ē), *iota* (i), and *upsilon* (u), along with the diphthongs *epsilon-iota* (ei) and *omicron-iota* (oi), all had the same sound. This caused considerable confusion in many words. It caused special problems in the first- and second-person personal pronouns in the plural number. Thus, in 1 John 1:4, many manuscripts read "your joy" while others read "our joy." The only difference is the first letter of the word. "Our" is *ēmōn*, and "your" is *umōn*, and the two words would have been pronounced exactly the same. The confusion of these words is frequent in the manuscripts.

Another example of confusion of sound is found in Romans 5:1. Most manuscripts read the indicative form, *echomen,* "we have," but a number of the older manuscripts read *echōmen,* the subjunctive, "let us go on having." The only difference between the two words is whether the second vowel is *omicron* (o) or *omega* (ō). The two would have been pronounced alike. In a similar way, *epsilon* (e) and the diphthong *alpha-iota* (ai) were the same in sound. Thus, in Galatians 4:18, some manuscripts have the infinitive *zēlousthai,* and others have the imperative, *zēlousthe.* Occasionally, there was confusion of consonants as well. In John 1:13, some manuscripts read *egennēthēsan* (from the verb "to beget" or "to bear"), and others read *egenēthēsan* (from the verb "to become"). The only difference between the form of the two words is the question whether *nu* (n) is repeated. The sound would have been the same.

Sometimes it seems that the scribe was betrayed by his memory as he copied. This type of error took many forms. It was common for a scribe to change the reading in a Gospel to agree with the reading of a similar passage from another Gospel which was better known to him. In many instances this resulted in passages being changed to agree with the Gospel of Matthew, which was the favorite Gospel in the early church. A good example of this is the model prayer as contained in Matthew 6:9–13 and Luke 11:2–4. Read these verses in the King James Version and then in a modern translation such as the Revised Standard Version. You will notice that in the King James Version the texts of the two Gospels are almost identical, while in the modern version there is a great difference between the two. Evidently, later scribes, since they were more familiar with Matthew's Gospel, changed Luke to agree with Matthew. Sometimes the borrowing took place in Matthew's Gospel. Some suggest this explains the reference to the Son in Matthew 24:36. Again, compare this verse with Mark 13:32, first in the King James Version and then in the more recent translation. In the King James Version, Matthew makes no reference to the Son as not knowing "that day or hour." However, in the other translation, it is stated that neither the angels *nor the Son* knows. If this did not drop out of the original text of Matthew because of the reluctance to admit the Son might not know some particular thing, it crept into Matthew from the scribe's familiarity with Mark. However, it is likely that the words do belong in Matthew's account and were lost in some manuscripts by accidental or intentional omission.

In a similar way, quotations from the Old Testament were sometimes adapted to make them agree more accurately with the text with which the scribe was familiar. In some copies of Matthew 15:8, scribes lengthened the quotation from Isaiah 29:13 to make it agree with the prophet's words. The same thing occurred in copies of Luke 4:18 and Acts 7:37. This type of harmonizing took place with regard to Ephesians and Colossians, letters probably written in close relation to each other by Paul. A few manuscripts add 'through his blood" in Colossians 1:14, probably borrowing the phrase from the parallel passage in Ephesians 1:7.

Other ways in which the memory might deceive led to the substitution of a synonym for the word that was actually in the text being copied. Different words for "said" are used in manuscripts of Matthew 22:37, and different words for "eyes" are used in Matthew 9:29. Changes of word order were probably often due to a lapse of memory, especially when the order of words did not change the basic meaning of the phrase being copied. Such variations of word order are frequent but ordinarily do not affect the meaning of the passage. A good example of such a change is 1 Corinthians 1:2. Many manuscripts read, "the church of God which is in Corinth, sanctified in Christ Jesus." Others read, "the church of God, sanctified in Christ Jesus, which is in Corinth."

It was easy for the scribe to shift the order of letters in a word, especially when he was copying from a manuscript which did not divide the letters into separate words. Of course, sometimes this resulted in altogether different words. In Mark 14:65 some manuscripts read *elabon*, "received." But others read *ebalon*, "threw." Such changes could result in readings that are nonsense but which slipped by the scribe as he was copying.

Another type of unintentional mistake could be classified as an error of judgment. At times the scribe had to make a choice, and the result was not always the best. One area where the scribe had to use his judgment was when he found something added in the margin of his manuscript. Corrections were often made on the margin, with the intention that these be placed in the text when a new copy was made. Other material might also be added in the margin, such as scribal notations or tradition known to the scribe. When the manuscript was later copied, the scribe had to decide whether these marginal notations were to be included in the newly copied manuscript. It is probable that some materials copied in this way were not an original part of the text. One such instance could be John 5:4, the reference to the angel's coming down and stirring the water in the pool in Jerusalem (as in KJV). This verse is missing in the older and better manuscripts of John. But since it could have been the popular understanding of the cause of the situation, a scribe put it in the margin, from which it was later copied into the text. Another example of the same type of occurrence may be Acts 8:37. There would have been added appeal at this point, for many would have considered it improper to baptize the man unless he had made an open confession of his faith in Jesus. Undoubtedly he made such a confession, but Luke probably did not include it when he wrote Acts.

An example where the scribe must not have paid any attention to what he was copying is found in 2 Corinthians 8:4. The words "that we receive" are added in some manuscripts at the end of the verse. This makes the verse read; ". . . of their own accord begging us earnestly to share in the grace and the fellowship of the ministry toward the saints which we received" (my translation). Then a later scribe probably added in the margin, "It is found thus in many of the copies." In one manuscript, the scribe placed these words in the text immediately following the words, "that we receive."[7] Certainly the reading makes no sense and could not have made sense to the scribe if he had been paying close attention to what he was doing. Instead, he was merely copying words. B. M. Metzger[8] cites another example where a scribe copied a text that was nonsense. The scribe was copying the genealogy of Jesus in Luke's Gospel from a manuscript which had the list of names in two columns. Instead of copying one column and then the second, the scribe copied across the two columns. One result is that in this manuscript God is claimed to have been the son of Aram!

In addition to these accidental variations, scribes were sometimes guilty of making intentional changes in the text of a manuscript. Since it may sound strange to call these intentional errors, it is better to say they were intentional changes. Indeed, these would introduce errors into the text, but it was not the intention of the scribe to do so, since he thought he was restoring the text to its original form. Sometimes these changes are simple and quite innocent, but at other times they introduce matters of some substance. They might be made by the scribe or by someone who corrected the work of the scribe. The ideal scribe would copy what was in the text from which he was working. But sometimes he considered the text to be wrong and made changes. In doing this, he might succeed in correcting an earlier error, but most often he simply introduced a new one. As B. M. Metzger points out: "Odd though it may seem, scribes who thought were more dangerous than those who wished merely to be faithful in copying what lay before them."[9]

Many of the changes were matters of form, spelling, and grammar. It was perhaps only natural for scribes to think that the New Testament writings must be in the best possible form. All too often, they measured form by that of the Greek classics, not realizing that such form was not used by the common people of the first century or by the writers of the New Testament. Variations in spelling also occurred. Sometimes this was because of the unfamiliarity of the word or name. Thus, in Luke 11:15, three forms of the name for the prince of demons is found: Beelzebul, Beelzebub, and Beezeboul. Where did Jesus encounter the demoniac in Mark 5:1? Was it in the country of the Gadarenes, the country of the Gergesenes, or the country of the Gerasenes? All three spellings of the word are found in manuscripts. What was the name of the pool in John 5:2? Manuscripts vary in giving the name, from Bethzatha to Bethesda, Bethsaida, and Belzatha.

Corrections in grammar are also found. The writings did not always measure up to the scribe's standards, or at least to his understanding of the rules of grammar. These corrections are especially common in the Book of Revelation, where the grammar is quite difficult. Often scribes "corrected" the grammar, and thus perhaps were defeating the purpose of the writer.

It is possible that corrections to make passages agree with a parallel in another Gospel or letter were intentional changes, although we cannot know whether these were accidental or intentional. In addition to the passages referred to above in the discussion of different types of unintentional error, there are similar changes in Acts 9:5–6. Materials from a parallel account of Paul's conversion have been inserted from Acts 26:14–15. In Matthew 27:49, words have been introduced in some early manuscripts from John 19:34 about the soldier who thrust his spear into the side of Jesus and brought forth a flow of blood and water.

Some changes were evidently made to clear up historical difficulties. In Mark 1:2, the evangelist begins a quotation which he states to be from "Isaiah, the prophet." Some observant scribe, however, noted that this quotation was actually from two books of the Old Testament: Isaiah and Malachi. In order that Mark might not be wrong, he changed the reading to "as it is written in the prophets." It is true that some explain this variation in another way. They suggest that the original text had only the quotation from Isaiah and that a later scribe added the portion from Malachi. Thus Mark was originally correct, and the problem arose because some scribe added to the original. But, even if this were so, another scribe then changed the original reference to Isaiah so that *his* text of Mark would not appear incorrect.

A variety of readings are found in Matthew 27:9. Most manuscripts read that the reference to the thirty pieces of silver is from Jeremiah. However, other scribes, perhaps having difficulty finding a suitable reference in Jeremiah, changed it to read Ezekiel or

Isaiah, and in some manuscripts no prophet is named at all. In John 1:28, Origen changed Bethany to Bethabara, evidently because he knew of no Bethany beyond the Jordan River. Origen's conjecture has been preserved in many of the manuscripts of this portion of John. In a similar way, some scribes changed John's reference to the sixth hour in the story of Jesus' trial, apparently to make it agree with Mark's reference to the third hour (John 19:14; Mark 15:25).

Sometimes a scribe was faced with making a choice between readings that appeared in two different manuscripts. When he could not decide which was correct, he included both readings in his text. Thus, in Luke 24:53, some manuscripts read "blessing God." Others read "praising God." But in a number of the later manuscripts, the reading "praising and blessing God" is found. Such readings occur with some frequency in the later manuscripts and are a sign of what Westcott and Hort call the Syrian text.

A final type of intentional change can be put under the heading of doctrinal corrections. While some have argued that such corrections never took place within the more "orthodox" section of the church, such claims seem to be without justification. From the late second century, it was noted that the heretics were changing the text. The best example of this is Marcion who altered the Gospel of Luke and the letters of Paul to fit his own theology.[10]

A few of the clearer examples of doctrinal correction can be cited. In Mark 9:29, Jesus had answered his disciples' question concerning the reason for their failure in healing the demon-possessed boy: "This kind cannot be driven out by anything but prayer" (RSV). When fasting became important in the life of the church, some scribe added to this statement the words "and fasting." The meaning of Jesus' teaching on almsgiving, prayer, and fasting was changed when a scribe added the word "openly" to the promise that God would reward the one who did these things in secret (Matt. 6:4,6,18). In Luke 23:32, the three oldest manuscripts read "they were leading other criminals, two, with him to be crucified." Later scribes changed this by reversing the word order of two words so that the reading became "two others, criminals," thus avoiding any possibility that Jesus might be thought of as a criminal. Scribes had much difficulty with references to Joseph and the parents of Jesus. In Luke 2:33, they changed the reading "his father and his mother" to read "Joseph and his mother." In Luke 2:43, the reference to "his parents" was changed in some manuscripts to read "Joseph and Mary." Reference has already been made to the 1522 edition of Erasmus, in which he added the reference to the three heavenly witnesses (1 John 5:8) on the basis of a single late Greek manuscript.

Scribes were only human and therefore made many mistakes in copying manuscripts. But we should be slow to criticize their work. If it had not been for their devotion and toil, our knowledge of the text of the New Testament would have been much more limited. They labored at the task of reproducing the story of the Good News with little human reward. When all has been said, we can affirm that the scribes have faithfully preserved for us the early materials relating to the text of the New Testament. Our greatest problems do not lie in their failures, but rather with the vast amount of material that has been preserved. The difficult task of the textual scholar is to sift through this material to determine what the New Testament writers originally put down on their scrolls. Because of the efforts of the scribes, this is possible to a degree that should be a source of amazement to all. We can have great confidence in the text of the New Testament that has been developed by the work of scholars through the centuries. It faithfully reproduces the original manuscripts to the extent that we need have no fears that future discoveries or study will call into question any cherished doctrine of our faith. However, the next task that lies before us is to see how the text which we use today has been developed, especially during the last century.

4

The Practice of Textual Study

Throughout the eighteenth and nineteenth centuries, men were developing the principles and discovering the materials which were to make possible the New Testament as we know it today. It was a difficult type of work which often met with strong opposition. Many were fearful lest the New Testament, as they knew it, should prove to be something other than the original text. They were afraid that the writing on which they had based their faith might prove to be false, or that some cherished belief might be questioned by textual study. In a sense, Mill started the process with his publication of a long list of variant readings. He made no attempt to evaluate these or to indicate any principles by which such a process could be undertaken.

It remained for Bengel to take the first decisive step forward. He indicated which variant readings were more likely to be correct, some being seen as the original reading, yet having to be placed in the margin of his text. He also was the first to divide manuscripts into families. He believed that groups of manuscripts were as closely related as human families, since they descended from an original common ancestor. A family has been defined as ". . . a group of MSS marked by distinctive characteristics and often connected with a particular locality like the members of a genealogical tree."[1] Bengel believed there were two families. The Asiatic was represented by the later manuscripts; the African by the earlier. In addition, Bengel insisted that it was not the number of manuscripts which supported a reading but the value of those manuscripts which should be considered in deciding which reading was original. Both Semler and Griesbach accepted the idea of three families. The theory of textual criticism was also moved forward considerably by the work of Griesbach.

The Genealogical Method

The two key figures in the history of the development of the text remain those of Brooke Foss Westcott and Fenton John Anthony Hort. They are of outstanding importance because with them the critical text became reality and the principles of criticism were set forth so clearly and effectively that their influence is still paramount in the field of textual study. As we shall see, some of their ideas have been modified by later scholars, but no new theory of criticism has been developed to replace the one they set forth. All of their work centered around one basic concept: "The first step towards obtaining a sure foundation is a consistent application of the principle that KNOWLEDGE OF DOCUMENTS SHOULD PRECEDE FINAL JUDGEMENT UPON READINGS."[2] Therefore, they concentrated upon the relationship between documents, the textual families, and upon the value of documents and groups of documents. Their work was issued in two volumes. Volume one contained their revised text. Volume two—introduction and appendix—represented the principles and methods used in developing their text. This second volume was written by Hort but represented conclusions agreed to by both men. Although it will be referred to in this chapter by the name of its author, Hort, it should be remembered that they were in full agreement.

Hort was convinced that manuscripts were related and that, in a sense, a family tree could be developed which showed the ancestry of various documents. He believed that this sort of historical relationship must be shown in order to develop any degree of confidence with regard to the text.

The vast majority of the manuscripts were eliminated as being of little value in the development of the text. Hort was convinced that virtually all the later uncial manuscripts and almost all the minuscules represented a text of the New Testament that could not be traced back earlier than the fourth century. This textual type was labeled Syrian, perhaps because it was believed to have its origin in Antioch of Syria. Hort thought it developed out of a conscious effort to incorporate the best from the extant manuscripts of the day. The other three textual traditions made contributions to the formation of this new text. Readings might be adopted from one text or another, and texts from two traditions would sometimes be combined. This type of combination, called conflation, is one of the signs of the late text. Such changes must have been the result of the work of editors who were deliberately setting out to make a text that would replace the many and varied texts being used at the time.

> The qualities which the authors of the Syrian text seem to have most desired to impress on it are lucidity and completeness. They were evidently anxious to remove all stumbling-blocks out of the way of the ordinary reader, so far as this could be done without recourse to violent measures. They were apparently equally desirous that he should have the benefit of instructive matter contained in all the existing texts, provided it did not confuse the context or introduce seeming contradictions. New omissions accordingly are rare, and where they occur are usually found to contribute to apparent simplicity. New interpolations on the other hand are abundant, most of them being due to harmonistic or other assimilation, fortunately capricious and incomplete. Both in matter and in diction the Syrian text is conspicuously a full text. It delights in pronouns, conjunctions, and expletives and supplied links of all kinds, as well as in more considerable additions.[3]

Hort was convinced that when only the Syrian text supported a reading, this reading could not be correct. It could not have originated earlier than the fourth century or it would have appeared in some earlier form of the text. We must remember that it was this Syrian text which lay behind the Received Text which ruled for over two centuries and from which the King James Version of the New Testament was translated.

A second and more important textual family is the Western. It was given this name because most of its remaining witnesses come from the western part of the Roman Empire. However, Hort admitted that this text was extremely ancient in origin and, at least in the beginning, was not confined to the West. This textual tradition can be traced back to the middle of the second century, the writings of the early Church Fathers scattered from Rome to the Middle East to Alexandria. It is represented by the Old Syriac and Old Latin versions, both of which had their beginnings in the second century.

> The chief and most constant characteristic of the Western readings is a love of paraphrase. Words, clauses, and even whole sentences were changed, omitted, and inserted with astonishing freedom, wherever it seemed that the meaning could be brought out with greater force and definiteness. They often exhibit a certain rapid vigour and fluency which can hardly be called a rebellion against the calm and reticent strength of the apostolic speech, for it is deeply influenced by it, but which, not less than a tamer spirit of textual correction, is apt to ignore pregnancy and balance of sense, and especially those meanings which are covered by exceptional choice or collocation of words.[4]

At times, the Western text appears to include material taken from traditional or even nonbiblical sources. This tendency toward change and expansion is especially noticeable in the text of Luke and Acts, where many additions are found in Western manuscripts. However, there are a few cases where the Western text, surprisingly, omits material that is found in all other textual traditions. For want of a better descriptive term, Hort referred to these as "Western non-interpolations." He was unwilling to admit that these passages were insertions into the Neutral text. Since the Western text is characterized by insertions, it is quite significant when it omits material found in other family traditions. Most of the Western noninterpolations occur in the last three chapters of

Luke's Gospel and were looked upon by Hort as probably the correct readings.[5] The chief representative of the Western text in the Gospels and Acts is Codex Bezae (D), along with the Latin tradition and the Old Syriac version. In Paul's letters, another bilingual manuscript, D_2, is the leading representative of the Western family.

A third text type identified by Hort was given the name Alexandrian. It was found only in fragmentary form, and no manuscript was believed to be a pure representative of this textual tradition.

> The changes made have usually more to do with language than matter, and are marked by an effort after correctness of phrase. They are evidently the work of careful and leisurely hands, and not seldom display a delicate philological tact which unavoidably lends them at first sight a deceptive appearance of originality.[6]

There remain a few manuscripts which do not seem to have been greatly influenced by any of the changes which led to the development of these three textual types. To these, Hort gave the name Neutral, and they were thought to contain the most ancient form of the text with the fewest changes. They are represented primarily by Codex Vaticanus (B) and Codex Sinaiticus, along with the Coptic versions. Of these, Hort looked upon B as having the purest text, except in the Pauline Epistles, in which he found evidence of a number of Western readings. On the other hand, Sinaiticus has some Western and Alexandrian readings throughout. Yet these two documents remain the chief witnesses to the original text.

It is in this area of family relationships that Westcott and Hort made their greatest contribution to the study of the New Testament text. They moved the study a major step beyond any who had preceded them. In spite of later developments, this aspect of their study cannot be ignored.

Internal Evidence

One might well ask how it was that Hort came to the conclusion that the Neutral text was the nearest to the original and that it was best represented by Vaticanus and Sinaiticus. He reached this conclusion by a rigid application of the principles of internal evidence to the study of documents. Evidence is of two categories, external and internal. External evidence is the witness of actual documents. Internal evidence is divided into two types, transcriptional and intrinsic. Transcriptional evidence involves the consideration of how a scribe worked and of the types of errors a copyist might make. Intrinsic evidence is the attempt to look at the passage from the viewpoint of the author and to choose the reading which most nearly approaches the thought pattern of the author. Since intrinsic evidence is the most subjective, it must be used with great caution.

The study of documents on the basis of internal evidence seems to narrow down to four basic principles of criticism. The first and most important is that the reading to be preferred is the one which best explains the origin of the other readings. Thus, in John 6:69, the confession of Peter is recorded in various forms. These include: "the Christ"; "the Christ, the Holy One of God"; "the Christ, the Son of the Living God"; and "the Holy One of God." The third reading parallels the account in Matthew 16 and may be assumed to have come into John because of a scribe's familiarity with Matthew's Gospel. It in no way can explain the origin of the fourth reading. The first reading, "the Christ," seems to have been derived from the third, and it can be recognized as a common title given to Jesus. The second, "the Christ, the Holy One of God," seems to be a combination of the first and fourth. Thus, only the fourth reading can explain the origin of the others. If it were original, one could see how the others arose. If any of the others were original, there is no good way of explaining the origin of the reading "the Holy One of God."

The second principle is that the more difficult reading is preferred to the easier reading. Since it is more likely that the difficult reading bothered the scribe, it was only natural for him to put the text in a form that was easier for him and, from his viewpoint, the form which would have been the original reading. Of course, one must always keep in mind that a scribe might accidentally make an error which makes the reading more difficult. This principle is applicable only in regard to intentional changes. But barring accidental error, it is usually best to adopt the more difficult reading if it makes sense in the context.

The third principle is that the shorter reading is to be preferred to the longer. This may sound strange to us, considering our tendency to condense everything from books to food. But ancient scribes seemed to avoid omitting anything and were more likely to add to the text than subtract from it. Again, there is a word of caution. It was always possible that material might be omitted by accident. But, as a general rule, it remains true that the shorter reading will usually be preferred. This principle can be seen in the preference of Hort for the Western noninterpolations.

A fourth principle is that the reading most characteristic of the author is to be preferred. This is intrinsic evidence, and its application requires a sensitive spirit and a thorough knowledge of the writing and its author. In practice, it is applied only when all the other methods fail to lead one to a firm conclusion.[7] In addition to all that has been said, Hort reminds us that a scribe might be moved ''by a much greater variety of impulse than is usually supposed.''[8]

Identifying the Best Manuscripts

To determine the relative value of a document, principles such as those described above must be applied to each variant reading in the document. At each point at which the manuscript differs from a standard text, the principles of criticism are applied and a tentative decision made as to whether or not the manuscript is correct. When all variations have been studied, it can be determined that a manuscript appears to preserve the correct reading in a certain percentage of the cases. In other instances, it appears to preserve a late and/or incorrect reading. If the manuscript preserves the preferred reading in a large proportion of the cases, it can be assumed to preserve an early and true text. If the opposite is the case, then it is a manuscript which has a late and inaccurate text. On the basis of this type of study, Hort came to the conclusion that Vaticanus and

Sinaiticus were the two manuscripts which best preserved the original text of the New Testament.

The same type of procedure can then be applied to groups of manuscripts. Hort insisted that this was perhaps the key to developing an accurate text. Each group of manuscripts must be treated and studied separately. This study led to the conclusion that when Vaticanus and Sinaiticus agree, they usually contain the original text. In addition, it was discovered that BL, BC, and Sinaiticus BDZ are sound groups.

The final step in identifying the best manuscripts is to determine which family usually represents the best or original text. This has already been brought out in the discussion of the characteristics of the various textual types that Hort identified. For him, the Neutral text is the most reliable. The Syrian is always to be rejected when it stands alone. While the Western preserves many ancient readings, it is not likely to be correct except in the matter of a few omissions. The Alexandrian is a polished text and cannot be accepted in preference to the Neutral. On the basis of this understanding of families, groups of documents, and individual documents, Westcott and Hort prepared their critical text which was published in 1881. It was a major advance in the study of the New Testament text and has served as the basis for the study that has gone on for the past one hundred years.

Steps in Practice

The actual practice of textual criticism always begins with a consideration of the external evidence, the manuscripts which support each variant reading. First, the attempt is made to discover which families stand behind each reading. Hort insisted that if the Neutral family is united in its support of a reading, that reading is almost certain to be original. If the Neutral family is divided, then the evidence of the Western and Alexandrian families is of greater importance. Next, groups of manuscripts are considered. If groups which have the reputation of being generally correct support a particular reading, that is likely to be the original. Finally, individual manuscripts are considered. On the basis of all this evidence, a tentative conclusion is reached as to which variant is to be considered the original reading or best text.

The next step is to consider the internal evidence. The principles of internal evidence are applied to see what light they shed upon the variants. It is hoped that the conclusion reached on the basis of internal evidence will agree with the conclusion that has been reached by examining manuscript evidence. When this occurs, one can have great confidence that this is the correct reading. If transcriptional evidence, however, disagrees with the external, then one must resort to intrinsic evidence to reach a conclusion. Of course, such a conclusion always has a great element of doubt. On the whole, however, most instances are rather secure.

> The proportion of words virtually accepted on all hands as raised above doubt is very great, not less, on a rough computation, than seven eighths of the whole. The remaining eighth therefore, formed in great part by changes of order and other comparative trivialities, constitutes the whole area of criticism. . . . the words in our opinion still subject to doubt only make up about one sixtieth of the whole New Testament. In this second estimate the proportion of comparatively trivial variations is beyond measure larger than in the former; so that the amount of what can in any sense be called substantial variation is but a small fraction of the whole residuary variation, and can hardly form more than a thousandth part of the entire text.[9]

Mixture

One fact which complicates the entire procedure, and which Hort recognized and admitted, is that no pure texts have been preserved—there has been mixture in every manuscript that has survived. Mixture means that material from one textual tradition has found its way into a manuscript which represents another textual family. This must always be kept in mind in the study of the text. Thus, while Hort saw B as by far the best single manuscript of the New Testament, he admitted that in many places it did not preserve the original reading. Even it had been corrupted, perhaps because readings from other traditions had been incorporated into its ancestor. Nevertheless, he believed that by the knowledge of documents and the application of the principles of internal evidence, he was able to spot and eliminate from the Neutral text those readings which were derived from mixture.

Response to Westcott and Hort

Not all scholars have been convinced that Westcott and Hort have provided all the answers in the study of the New Testament text. At first, there were some who were bitter in their opposition, but gradually it became clear that the two men had discovered the correct basic principles. Much has been done during the past century that has led to further advancement and refinement. One of the extremely important areas of advance has involved the discovery and study of new materials. Hort knew nothing of any New Testament papyri, as these were not discovered until a number of years after his text was completed. And the most important of these finds were not made until fairly recent times. Therefore, the implications to be drawn from this evidence, which would inevitably influence decisions about texts and text types, were unknown to him. In addition, much effort has been put into the study of some manuscripts which were almost totally neglected in previous times.

The result of this continued study has been a shift in the understanding of families. Hort's terminology has been partially abandoned in favor of new family designations. New titles have been given to the families, owing primarily to the work of B. H. Streeter.[10] What Hort called the Neutral family is now known as the Alexandrian. His Alexandrian family is now called the Caesarean. The Western family has retained its Western designation, but the Syrian is now known as the Byzantine. One reason for the shift in terminology was the feeling that the use of the term Neutral was prejudicial since it gave the impression that this family represented a pure text, uninfluenced by error and change. Now a geographical designation has been given to that family, and the use of the text can be substantiated in the area centered in Alexandria. The name Caesarean is used in place of Hort's Alexandrian because it was thought for a time that the first indication of the existence of this textual tradition was in the writings of Origen after he moved from Alexandria to Caesarea.[11] The term Byzantine better describes the other text (Syrian), since it became prevalent in the Byzantine period.

For the most part, the family alignments remained unchanged. The Alexandrian family is best represented by B and Sinaiticus. The Western is represented by D, the Latin tradition, and the Old Syriac. The Byzantine is, like the Syrian of Hort, represented by most of the later manuscripts. It is only with the Caesarean that new discoveries changed the picture. Through the work of such men as B. H. Streeter, K. Lake, and W. H. Ferrar, certain resemblances were found in various Greek manuscripts. This involved especially p[45], Codex Koridethi (Theta), family 1 and family 13. It was discovered, at least in Mark, that these manuscripts were of the same textual tradition. As already mentioned, because it was first believed that Origen began to use this text only after his move to Caesarea, it was given the name Caesarean. Additional study has raised serious question as to whether this should be called a textual family or perhaps simply a textual tradition. In fact, there is the possibility that one should speak of a pre-Caesarean text and a Caesarean text. However, there is still some common ground among the manuscripts and further study will perhaps clarify their relationships.[12]

Much work has gone into the study of the Western and Byzantine families. Scholars today are no longer so confident as Hort that these families can be ignored when they are not supported by the Alexandrian or Caesarean texts. The assumption now is that it is possible for an original reading to have been retained by one of these families even though it has been lost in the other texts. F. G. Kenyon has pointed out one aspect of recent textual study.

> But it is also becoming increasingly recognized that the later text has preserved here and there ancient readings which have largely disappeared from other branches of the tradi-

tion, and which otherwise have only slight attestation among early witnesses, or even none at all.[13]

Thus, these two families must be taken seriously in any effort to develop the original text.

Doubts about the Genealogical Method

Another development of significance has been a reaction away from the genealogical approach advocated by Hort, some of whose successors looked upon this as the final answer to all questions. Since it was applied in a mechanical way, which was never envisioned by Hort, the result was a one-sided approach to the whole field of textual study. Today, while many still retain a wholesome attitude toward the study of manuscript relations, others have almost totally abandoned this approach. F. G. Kenyon remarks:

> We may put the matter in another way by saying that the genealogical method has proved to be of much more limited application in tracing the early history of the New Testament text than would appear from Westcott and Hort's theory. The method assumes the prior existence of a limited number of archetypes at no great distance from the original text, from which the main lines of tradition are descended, and that these archetypes can be reconstructed. But the extreme paucity of the surviving early witnesses . . . makes such a reconstruction impossible.[14]

Scholars today recognize that mixture was far more pronounced between the various textual types than Hort ever imagined. B. B. Warfield expressed the problem when he stated:

> The application of genealogical evidence to the New Testament has proved to be exceptionally difficult. Not only has the critic to face here an unheard-of abundance of matter, all of which has to be sifted and classified; but the problem is complicated by an unparalleled amount of mixture, which has reigned so universally that it has left scarcely a half-dozen witnesses entirely unaffected by it.[15]

Even this last assessment may be overly optimistic. It is likely that no manuscript is completely unmixed. Textual readings have crossed over all lines, from the earliest date from which manuscripts have been found.

In addition, manuscript discoveries in this century have shown that all of the major textual families must have been circulating in Egypt before the close of the second century. Such a realization casts new light on the entire theory of manuscript relations and the preservation of the text.

Rational Criticism

The result has been the development of what is known as the "eclectic" method, or "rational" criticism. It has grown out of what E. J. Epp calls the twentieth-century interlude in New Testament textual study.[16] He sets forth a number of indications that we are in a time between great achievements in the past and, hopefully, equally great achievements in the future. One sign is that no real progress in developing popular critical editions of the Greek New Testament has occurred since the work of Westcott and Hort in 1881. The two basic texts used today, which in their latest editions are identical in text, are very similar to the text of Westcott and Hort. Furthermore, Epp asks whether it is adequate to have as our "best" New Testament text one which is in reality more than ninety years old. He notes that the text of Westcott and Hort was based on no papyrus documents, on perhaps 45 uncials, on about 150 minuscules, and on a small number of lectionaries, in contrast to the much more abundant quantity of these materials available today.[17]

Another indication is that little progress has been made in textual theory since the time of Westcott and Hort. No theory has been presented which can show the development of the text in the earliest centuries. and no adequate understanding has developed with regard to the alterations that were made in the text during that time. Epp agrees with Hort that the text groups which can be shown to be pre-Byzantine are certainly closer to the original than the Byzantine text. But he claims that the decision that the Neutral is closer to the original than the Western was based on subjective grounds rather than on scientific, objective criteria.[18]

Another indication of an interlude is a renewed emphasis upon the Received Text. There are some today who argue that the late manuscripts, which contain that text, are the best manuscripts. There seems to be no justifiable basis upon which to make such a claim.[19]

As a result of all that has taken place in the last century, perhaps the most popular method of textual study today is the rational, a term indicating that the problem is reasoned out. J. N. Birdsall points out that the change which has taken place in this century is "to a method which views them [texts] in the context of history, and relates the changes observable in them to known points in the history of their study and interpretation."[20] This means that it is impossible to trace the descent of manuscripts with any great degree of confidence. All manuscripts are mixed, and we cannot know for certain their interrelation.

Those who practice rational criticism are not in total agreement as to procedure. Some say that it makes no difference what manuscript supports a reading, and that external evidence must be ignored. The quality of different manuscripts and families is disregarded. "This kind of 'eclecticism' becomes the great leveller—all variants are equals and equally candidates for the original text, regardless of date, residence, lineage, or textual context."[21] Fortunately, we are not driven to that extreme, and most followers of rational criticism are more moderate. Manuscript evidence must be considered, but it does not have the final word. No one textual type can be shown to be superior at every point. The original may be preserved in only one or a few manuscripts, even late manuscripts. It may have vanished from the Greek manuscripts and appear only in a version. This idea would never have been approved by Westcott and Hort. They believed that the Byzantine family never preserved the true text when it stood alone. However, Birdsall points out that "no genealogical method can lead us to the original text. An informed recensional activity must take place and a text be provisionally established.''[22] Kenyon describes rational criticism when he states:

> Since, as we have seen, no manuscript or group is infallible, it follows that the original reading may have survived in any part of the tradition, and consequently all variants must be considered on their merits, and not, e.g. set aside at the outset as 'late' (which may mean no more than that the manuscript attestation is late), or as occurring only in the versions, nor on the other hand given undue consideration because they appear in certain authorities or combinations of them. That reading will be chosen which, after consideration of all relevant factors, best explains the emergence of the other variants.[23]

The basic principle used in the practice of rational criticism is that the reading which best explains the origin of the other readings is most likely to be correct. We have already seen that this was one of the principles used in the study of internal evidence, and most scholars today would agree that it is the key criterion to be applied when studying a textual problem. The practice of moderate rational criticism does not lead to uncertainty. However, continued study in methods is necessary in order that we may have assurance about the exact text of the New Testament to be studied and followed.

It is impossible to predict with any degree of confidence what may happen in the immediate future with regard to the text of the New Testament. Additional early witnesses to the text may be discovered, although it is not likely that any will be found which will greatly change the text with which we are familiar. However, such witnesses may enable us better to understand the history of the text and the relationship of manuscripts. It seems more likely that the future will see refinement of methods. The result may be a text greatly similar to our present one, but, by the use of such methods, greater confidence will be placed in the results. However, we should realize that our present text is a good text and need have no fears that any important doctrine will be threatened by future discoveries or further work. We can be assured that the translations based upon the text of Nestle-Aland and the United Bible Societies are based upon readings that give us the basic message of the original authors. And it is this message which we seek, for it is upon this message that we base our faith and practice. We can be grateful that God has been at work preserving the Word which he inspired.

5

Examples of Variant Readings

All the explanations in the world can never take the place of actual practice and example. Therefore, it seems best to work through some specific textual problems. This will enable the reader to see the way in which the work is carried out, thereby understanding why certain readings appear in the New Testament text in contrast to others which are rejected or placed only in a footnote. Of course, since such examples are almost without number, some principle has to be used in the selection of the ones to be included in such a work as this. It seems best to use examples which might come to the attention of the observant reader of the New Testament. For the most part, the passages referred to in this chapter are those where clear differences can be seen when one compares the King James Version with a modern translation. This has not been done to cast doubts upon the King James Version, which is a good translation of a text that was the best available at the time. This principle has been adopted since it seems to be the clearest and least confusing. The differences will be obvious in each instance. Why are they present? On what basis have later editors made the decision to change the reading which was used for so many centuries? It is hoped that this process will demonstrate how these decisions were made and will show that the editors were honest and dedicated in their work.

Manuscript Witness by Family

Before we begin consideration of these examples, it will be helpful to provide a list of the most important manuscripts which support the various textual families. This will save much time and space as we look at the various passages. It will be easier if we divide the witnesses into categories. First, we will look at the families as they appear in manuscripts of the Gospels.

The *Alexandrian* witnesses in the Gospels include:

B (Vaticanus), fourth century, located in the Vatican Library in Rome.

Aleph (Sinaiticus), fourth century, now in the British Museum, London.

C (Ephraemi Rescriptus), fifth century, now in the National Library, Paris. Although this manuscript is quite old, it is not as important as some other manuscripts because it contains a number of late, Byzantine readings.

L (Regius), eighth century, also in the National Library, Paris.

T (Borgianus), fifth century, now in Rome.

W (Washington), fifth century, in the Smithsonian Library, Washington, D.C. This manuscript represents the Alexandrian family in Luke 1:1–8:12 and John 5:12–21:25.

Z (Dublinensis), sixth century, Trinity College, Dublin.

Delta (Sangallensis), ninth century, at St. Gall, Switzerland. This manuscript is Alexandrian in Mark only.

Psi (Laurensis), eighth or ninth century, in a monastery on Mt. Athos, Greece. This manuscript is Alexandrian in Mark but only partially so in Luke and John.

p66 (Bodmer II), about A.D. 200, Geneva.

p75 (Bodmer XIV, XV), A.D. 175–225, Geneva.

Minuscule manuscript 33, ninth century, Paris. This is considered to be the best of the minuscules in the Gospels.

Minuscule manuscript 892, ninth or tenth century, British Museum, London.

Minuscule manuscript 1241, twelfth or thirteenth century, Mt. Sinai.

In addition, the Coptic versions are a secondary witness to this textual family, although these versions will often contain readings from other textual types.

B, Aleph, C, and Psi are witnesses to the Alexandrian text in Acts. There are other manuscripts that join this family in Acts:

A (Alexandrinus), fifth century, British Museum, London, a major witness to the Alexandrian text except in the Gospels.

p^{45} (Chester Beatty Papyrus I), early third century, in the Chester Beatty Museum, Dublin, and the National Library, Vienna.

For the writings of Paul, we have B, Aleph, A, C, and Psi. Other Alexandrian witnesses include:

H_3 (Euthalianus), sixth century, scattered in a number of libraries in Europe.

I (Washingtonianus II), sixth century, in the Smithsonian Library, Washington, D.C.

One additional papyrus needs to be added to our list for Paul's letters: p^{46} (Chester Beatty Papyrus II), about A.D. 200, in the Chester Beatty Museum, Dublin, and the University of Michigan Library, Ann Arbor.

For the General Epistles, the major Alexandrian witnesses are B, Aleph, A, C, and Psi.

In Revelation, the primary witnesses to this family are A, Aleph, C, and P. Also, p^{47} (Chester Beatty Papyrus III), late third century, Chester Beatty Museum, Dublin, is a less important witness to this same textual family.

The *Caesarean* textual tradition has been identified only in the Gospels, primarily in Mark. Therefore, we are concerned about its witnesses only in these books. We will make no effort to distinguish, as some do, between a pre-Caesarean text and a Caesarean text. The major witnesses to this text are:

p^{45} (Chester Beatty Papyrus I).

W (Washington), in Mark 5:31–16:20.

Theta (Koridethi), ninth century, now at Tiflis.

Family 1 and family 13, groups of minuscule manuscripts.

Other minuscule manuscripts usually identified with the Caesarean text are 565, ninth century, in Leningrad, and 700, eleventh century, in the British Museum, London.

The Armenian and Georgian versions are also secondary witnesses to this text.

The *Western* text is supported in the Gospels by:

D (Bezae), fifth or sixth century, University Library, Cambridge.

W (Washington), in Mark 1:1–5:30.

The Old Latin, the Old Syriac, the Diatessaron of Tatian, and most of the early Fathers.

In Acts, we can add E_2 (Laudianus), sixth century, Bodleian Library, Oxford. Some small papyrus fragments also support this text.

In Paul's letters, the main witnesses are:

D_2 (Claromontanus), sixth century, National Library, Paris.

F_2 (Augiensis), ninth century, Trinity College, Cambridge.

G_3 (Boernerianus), ninth century, National Library, Dresden.

Old Latin manuscripts and the early Fathers also support this family in Paul's writings.

In the General Epistles, the major witnesses are the Old Latin manuscripts. In Revelation, no specific Western witnesses have been identified.

As has been stated earlier, most of the late uncial manuscripts and almost all the minuscules are witnesses for the Byzantine text. The major uncial manuscripts include, in the Gospels:

A (Alexandrinus).

E (Basiliensis), eighth century, University Library, Basel, Switzerland.

F (Boreelianus), ninth century, University Library, Utrecht, Netherlands.

G (Seidelianus), ninth century, British Museum, London.

H (Seidelianus II), ninth century, Hamburg City Library.

K (Cyprius), ninth century, National Library, Paris.

P (Guelpherbytanus), sixth century, Wölfenbüttel.

S (Vaticanus II), 949, Vatican Library, Rome.

V (Mosquensis), ninth century, in Moscow.

W (Washington), in Matthew; Luke 8:13–24:53; and John 1:1–5:12.

Pi (Petropolitanus), ninth century, Leningrad.

Omega (Dionysiacus), ninth century, Mt. Athos, Greece.

In Acts, the major representatives of the Byzantine text are:

H_2 (Mutinensis), ninth century, at Modena, Italy.

L_2 (Angelicus), ninth century, Angelica Library, Rome.

P_2 (Porphyrianus), ninth century, Leningrad.

The chief representative in Paul and the General Epistles is L_2.

Readings from the Gospels

We will first consider readings from the Gospels. Matthew 5:22 reads in part in the King James Version: ". . . whosoever is angry with his brother without a cause. . . ." The Revised Standard Version reads: ". . . every one who is angry with his brother. . . ." Modern translations leave out any reference to the words *without a cause*. The manuscript evidence favoring the omission of the words (actually only one word in Greek, *eikēi*) are: Alexandrian—p[67], Aleph (original), B; Western—Vulgate. Manuscripts which include the word are: Alexandrian—L, minuscules 33, 892, 1241, Coptic; Caesarean—Theta, family 1, family 13, minuscules 565, 700; Western—D, Old Latin, and Old Syriac; Byzantine—a corrector of Aleph, K, W, Delta, Pi, almost all minuscules, and the later Syriac.[1]

We look first at the external evidence. The major representatives of the Alexandrian family agree in support of the omission. All three of the other families agree on including the word. According to the study of Westcott and Hort, B and Aleph are to be considered the best group. In addition, when individual manuscripts are considered, it is probable that B is the best witness and Aleph next best. However, since these are the only major manuscripts which support this reading, external evidence cannot give us a final answer. So we must look at the internal evidence. The first principle is that the reading to be preferred is the one which best explains the origin of other readings. If the word was included in the original, there seems to be no reason that would lead a scribe to omit it unless it was by accidental oversight. However, there would be a tendency to include some such qualifying word. The statement of Jesus seems so absolute. He gives no excuse for being angry with one's brother. This is harsh, and the temptation is always to soften such rigorous demands. It may be that the word was added on the margin of some manuscript and then copied into the text. The scribe might have been familiar with Psalm 69:4, "They that hate me without a cause . . . are more than the hairs of mine head . . ." (KJV). Applying the second and third principles—the shorter reading and the more difficult reading—also supports the omission of the word. Insofar as intrinsic evidence is concerned, Jesus' teachings are usually absolute, and we might expect him to give such a command as this without any qualification of it at all. On the basis of all the evidence, it seems that the words *without cause* did not appear in the original of this verse.

In Matthew 6:4, is found the statement: ". . . thy Father which seeth in secret himself shall reward thee openly" (KJV). Most recent translations leave out the word *openly*. The omission of the word is supported by: Alexandrian—Aleph, B, Z, 33, Coptic; Caesarean—family 1, family 13; Western—D, some Old Latin manuscripts, Vulgate, one Old Syriac. The word is found in: Alexandrian—L, 892, 1241; Caesarean—Theta, 565, 700; Western—most Old Latin manuscripts, one Old Syriac; Byzantine— K, W, Delta, Pi, most minuscules, and most of the Syriac version.

In this instance, we find the major manuscripts of the Alexandrian family joined by the leading representative of the Western text and two of the leading representatives of the Caesarean. This means that the manuscript evidence itself leans strongly to the omission of the word. In this case, it is easier to suppose that the word (actually three words in Greek) would have been added by the scribe rather than omitted. The words would not have bothered him if they had been in the text, but their absence would be a different matter. The scribe might have been troubled by the fact that no one would be able to see God's vindication of the righteous man if the words were not present. Again, the shorter reading supports the omission. In this case, intrinsic evidence also strongly supports the omission. If the words are included, they seem to contradict what Jesus had been teaching about the motive for giving to the poor. The same textual problem occurs at the end of verse 6 with similar manuscript evidence, and at the close of verse 18 with overwhelming manuscript support for the shorter reading.

Mark 1:2 begins: "As it is written in the prophets . . ." (KJV). Another translation reads: "It is written in Isaiah the prophet . . ." (NIV). While there are variations with regard to the use of the definite article before the name Isaiah, on the whole the following manuscripts support the reference to Isaiah: Alexandrian— Aleph, B, L, Delta, 33, 892, 1241, part of the Coptic; Caesarean—Theta, family 1, 565, 700; Western—D, the Latin tradition, most of the Syriac. Manuscripts which read "in the prophets" include: Caesarean—family 13; Byzantine—A, K, P, W, Pi, and most minuscules.

In this verse, the Alexandrian, Western, and most of the Caesarean support the reading "Isaiah the prophet." Only the Byzantine and part of the Caesarean give support to the other reading. The best groups and the best individual manuscripts also support the reference to Isaiah. Thus, external evidence gives strong support to the reading found in recent translations, and when we turn to internal evidence, we find much the same thing to be true. The reference to Isaiah best explains the origin of the other reading. If the scribe were observant, he would realize that the quotation before him was partly from Isaiah and partly from Malachi. He would be tempted to change the citation to make it agree with the quotation. However, if "the prophets" had been original, there would have been no recognizable reason for the scribe to make the changes. Certainly the reference to Isaiah is the more difficult reading. Therefore, the reading "Isaiah the prophet" must be assumed to have been original. As previously mentioned, it is true that some would argue that Mark had originally quoted only from Isaiah, and a later scribe added the reference from

Malachi. However, there is no manuscript evidence to support this idea, and it is best not to resort to conjecture in determining the New Testament text.

One of the problem passages that has generated much discussion is the conclusion of the Gospel of Mark. The King James Version includes 16:9–20 as part of the text. The first edition of the Revised Standard Version placed these verses in a note at the bottom of the page. The words are included in brackets in the *New American Standard Bible*. *The New International Version* separates them from the body of the Gospel by a horizontal line. The evidence is more complex here because, besides the reading which appears as verses 9–20, there is also a shorter ending that appears in some manuscripts. Also, one manuscript has a long insertion at the end of verse 14. Verses 9–20 are omitted by: Alexandrian—Aleph, B, some Coptic manuscripts; Western—one Old Syriac manuscript; Byzantine—one minuscule. In addition, Clement of Alexandria and Origen both witness to manuscripts that ended Mark after 16:8. These may have been Alexandrian or Western in nature. A number of minuscule manuscripts include verses 9–20 but indicate by markings that there is question about whether they belong in the text. Only the shorter ending appears in one Old Latin manuscript. The longer ending, verses 9–20, is included in: Alexandrian—C, Delta, 33, 892, some Coptic; Caesarean—W, Theta, family 13, 565, 700; Western—D, the Latin tradition, one Old Syriac manuscript; Byzantine—A, K, X, Pi, most minuscules, most Coptic. Some manuscripts include both the longer and the shorter endings: Alexandrian—L, Psi, part of the Coptic version.

It can be seen that Aleph and B, the main representatives of the Alexandrian text, stand together in support of the ending of Mark at 16:8. The other families support the inclusion of verses 9–20. However, the presence of another, shorter, ending raises some questions. Manuscript evidence suggests that the verses in question were not part of the Gospel as Mark wrote it. Does internal evidence give the same answer? If the verses were original, there was no reason for a scribe to omit them. There was nothing in them which would have bothered him to any great extent. However, if his manuscript had ended at verse 8, he might well have felt something else was needed. The great problem was that no resurrection appearances had been presented. And thus there would have been a temptation to supply what seemed to the scribe to be a more adequate ending. In this case, the principles of the shorter reading and the more difficult reading both support the end of the Gospel of Mark at 16:8.

Many would raise questions on the basis of the author's intent, since they do not believe that Mark could have planned to end his Gospel in this way. It differs so much from the ending of Matthew and Luke that it does not seem possible that Mark could have had such a different plan and approach. So the suggestion is often made, even by those who believe that our present text must end at 16:8, that the original ending of Mark has been lost. It is indeed possible that the last portion of the manuscript was torn off, especially if it was in book form. However, this must have occurred with the most primitive copy, since no manuscript evidence exists to indicate what the ending might have been. It is recognized that almost all the material in 16:9–20 appears to be drawn from the resurrection accounts in the other Gospels and from experiences, particularly of Paul, as found in the Book of Acts. Textual criticism cannot tell us whether Mark originally ended his Gospel at 16:8. It can state that the textual materials which still exist show that the original text ends at 16:8 on the basis of the evidence now available. We should note that we lose nothing of value if we admit this to be true. All of value in these verses is found elsewhere in the New Testament. It is also worthy of note that verses 9–20 must have been added at a very early date, since they appear in the earliest versions, probably translated before the end of the second century.

Luke 2:14, since it is part of the Christmas story, is very familiar to most of us. It reads: "Glory to God in the highest, and on earth peace, good will toward men" (KJV). However, we also read: "Glory to God in the highest, And on earth peace among men with whom He is pleased!" (NASB). The two readings exist because of the difference in one word in the Greek text, in one instance a nominative case and in the other a genitive. Actually, there is only one letter different in the two words (*eudokia* is the nominative as used in the King James Version, *eudokias* is the genitive as used in the *New American Standard Bible*). The reading "with whom He is pleased" is supported by: Alexandrian—Aleph (original), B (original), W, Coptic manuscripts; Western—D, Old Latin, Vulgate; Byzantine—A. The other reading, "good will toward men," has the following manuscript support: Alexandrian—L, 892, 1241, Coptic manuscripts; Caesarean—Theta, family 1, family 13, 565, 700; Western-Old Syriac; Byzantine—corrector of Aleph, corrector of B, K, P, Delta, Psi, most minuscules, the later Syriac.

The former reading ("with whom He is pleased") has the support of the Alexandrian and Western families. The other reading is supported by the Caesarean and Byzantine. The better manuscripts also support the reading "with whom He is pleased." Thus, external evidence gives strong support to this version. Internal evidence gives support to the reading as well. It is likely that the genitive must be considered the more difficult reading. It suggests that God's peace does not come on all people, but only on those who receive his approval. However, it is also possible that the change was brought about by accident, since the final letter, *sigma*, could have been easily overlooked in the process of copying. However, it appears certain that the original copy of Luke read "with whom He is pleased."

Another variant occurs in Luke 2:33. "And Joseph and his mother marvelled . . ." (KJV)—"The child's father and mother marveled . . ." (NIV). Did Luke write of Joseph as the father of Jesus? "The child's father and mother" is supported by: Alexandrian—Aleph, B, L, W, 1241, some Coptic manuscripts; Caesarean—family 1, 700; Western—D, one Old Latin manuscript, Vulgate, Old Syriac. "Joseph and his mother" is read in: Alexandrian—33, 892, some Coptic manuscripts; Caesarean—Theta, family 13, 565; Western—the Old Latin; Byzantine—A, K, X, Delta, Pi, Psi, most minuscules, later Syriac. Other variations also appear. "Joseph his father and his mother" is read in one minuscule and the Ethiopic version. "His parents" appears in some Vulgate manuscripts. Some Syriac manuscripts make reference only to "Joseph" or "his father." These readings with only minor support can be eliminated except as they may suggest the existence of one or the other of the two major readings.

"The child's father and mother" is found in the Alexandrian family, the chief representative of the Western text, and one part of the Caesarean. "Joseph and his mother" is supported by the versions of the Western text, the rest of the Caesarean, and the Byzantine. External evidence gives support to "The child's father and mother." Internal evidence leans the same way. The reading "The child's father and mother" appears best to explain the origin of the other readings. It can be seen why a scribe might change the reference to "his father" to read "Joseph." However, there seems to be no reason why the change would be made in the opposite direction. Certainly, "The child's father and mother" is the more difficult reading. It would have bothered a scribe to refer to Joseph as in any sense the actual father of Jesus. Of course, we understand that this is not what the reference meant for Luke. Joseph was the legal father and, in the minds of many people of that day, was the actual father. Luke evidently was merely using the normal way people referred to Jesus and to his family relations during his lifetime. As time passed, there was an increased desire to protect the uniqueness of Jesus, and this would have led to change in the text. It appears, without any serious doubt, that Luke wrote "The child's father and mother."

Earlier in our discussion of the tendencies of textual families, reference was made to "Western non-interpolations." These are places where the reading is omitted by the Western text but included in all other witnesses. One such example is Luke 22:19b–20. A footnote in the Revised Standard Version indicates that these verses are omitted in "other authorities." The *New English Bible* omits the words, and *Today's English Version* includes them in brackets. The only manuscripts that omit the material are D and some Old Latin manuscripts, all Western witnesses. All other manuscripts include the words. Due to the tendency of the Western text to add material, Hort believed that where the Western omitted material, it was probably reproducing the original text. Scholars today are more hesitant to agree with this position. External evidence strongly supports the inclusion of the words in the text. Internal evidence is divided. The principles of preference for the shorter reading and the more difficult reading both support the omission of the words. The fact that Luke so clearly differed from the accounts in Mark, Matthew, and 1 Corinthians would have led scribes to desire to insert the reading. On this basis, the omission could explain the origin of the other reading. The scribe would have added it because he believed it needed to be present, and he derived it from other sources. However, it is possible that the omission came about by accident. Four identical words just before the omission and toward the end of verse 20 could have caused the eyes of a scribe to skip from the first occurrence of the words to the second occurrence. This would have led to the omission of all the material in between. What would Luke likely have written? Since his account of the Last Supper seems to be influenced by a tradition somewhat close to Paul's account in 1 Corinthians, it appears likely that his tradition would have included the material found in verses 19b–20. On the basis of all the evidence, it appears that it is best to include it in the text.

Another variant in Luke is to be considered. "Father, forgive them; for they know not what they do" (23:34, KJV). A footnote may be found in recent translations to indicate that other ancient authorities omit these words. They are omitted by: Alexandrian— p[75], B, W, 1241, Coptic manuscripts; Caesarean—Theta; Western—D (original), two Old Latin manuscripts, one Old Syriac manuscript; Byzantine—a corrector of Aleph. The words are included by: Alexandrian—Aleph (original), C, L, 33, 892, Coptic manuscripts; Caesarean—family 1, family 13, 565, 700; Western—most Old Latin manuscripts, Vulgate, one Old Syriac manuscript; Byzantine—A, a corrector of D, K, X, Delta, Pi, Psi, most minuscules, later Syriac.

For the first time, we discover that the leading representatives of the Alexandrian family are divided. Aleph supports the inclusion of the words, while B supports the omission. However, p^{75}, the oldest copy of Luke in existence, also supports the omission of the words. The chief representatives of the Western text and the Caesarean text support the omission. The words are included in other members of the Western family, other members of the Caesarean family, and the Byzantine.

On the basis of external evidence, no decision is possible. Which reading best explains the origin of other readings? Arguments could be given both ways. The principle of the shorter reading supports the omission of the words. Which reading is more difficult? It is hard for us to put ourselves back into the position of the scribe. It may be that the inclusion of the words was the more difficult reading from his viewpoint. He would not believe it proper for Jesus to pray for those who were killing him. Or he may have believed that the prayer was not answered, for did not God allow Jerusalem to be destroyed? If this was the scribe's viewpoint, he would not want the words to remain in his text.

On the other hand, if the words were not in the original, the scribe would not have felt any great need to insert them. The quality of forgiveness has never been a strong factor in the lives of people, and it is a difficult attribute to cultivate. It is extremely doubtful that a scribe would have invented the saying and placed it on the lips of Jesus. This means there can be little question that the saying does go back to Jesus.

However, whether it was an original part of Luke's Gospel is a different matter, and it is a borderline decision as to whether to include or exclude the reading. It is without doubt a saying of Jesus, but it may have come from oral tradition into this place in Luke's account. At this point, our emotions may have an influence, since we would feel a great loss if we had to surrender this saying. Thus, one is inclined to retain it in the text because its teaching is so important to us—but to do this with the realization that no certainty can be felt about the decision.

There are a number of textual variants of interest in John's Gospel. The first one to be considered is John 1:18. The King

James Version reads "the only begotten Son," and the Revised Standard Version reads "the only Son." However, the *New American Standard Bible* reads "the only begotten God." Another translation retains both God and Son: "God the only Son" (NIV). The question is whether the original reading was "Son" or "God." "God" is read by: Alexandrian—p^{66}, p^{75}, Aleph, B, C (original), L, 33, Coptic manuscripts. "The only Son" is read by: Alexandrian—892, 1241; Caesarean—Theta, family 1, family 13, 565, 700; Western—Old Latin, Vulgate, Old Syriac; Byzantine—A, a corrector of C, K, W, X, Delta, Pi, Psi, most minuscules. One Old Latin manuscript reads "only Son of God."

We see that "God" is read by the Alexandrian family, and "Son" is read by the Western, Caesarean, and Byzantine families. External evidence points toward "God" as the original reading. "God" seems to be the reading which most likely explains the origin of other readings. No scribe would have been bothered by the reading "Son." It was common to refer to Jesus in that way. However, there are few instances in the New Testament where Jesus is given the title "God" without any qualification. It could have caused the scribe to change the reading, either by accident or by intention, to the more normal term. "God" would have been the more difficult reading also. To call Jesus the "only God," or "unique God," might have appeared to threaten the role of the Father. The term "only Son" (only begotten Son) occurs elsewhere in this Gospel. Would John have used the title "God" to refer to Jesus? He does it one other time (20:28). Thus, intrinsic evidence supports the reading "God" which, on the basis of all evidence, seems to have been original.

Earlier, reference was made to the different readings found in John 6:69. "And we believe and are sure that thou art that Christ, the Son of the living God" (KJV)—". . . and we have believed, and have come to know, that you are the Holy One of God" (RSV). Almost all recent translations read "the Holy One of God." Manuscript support of the reading "the Holy One of God" is: Alexandrian—p^{75}, Aleph, B, C (original), L, W, Coptic manuscripts; Western—D, one Old Latin manuscript. "The Christ, the

Holy One of God" is read by: Alexandrian—p^{66}, some Coptic manuscripts. "The Son of God" is supported by: Western—one Old Latin and one Old Syriac manuscript. "The Son of the living God" is the reading in one minuscule manuscript. "The Christ, the Son of God" is found in: Alexandrian—33; Caesarean— Theta (original), family 1, 565; Western—a large part of the Latin tradition, one Old Syriac manuscript; Byzantine—one minuscule. "The Christ, the Son of the living God" is read by: Alexandrian— 892, 1241, Coptic manuscripts; Caesarean—family 13, 700; Western—some Old Latin manuscripts; Byzantine—a corrector of C, K, Delta, a corrector of Theta, Pi, Psi, most minuscules, later Syriac.

The major readings are "the Holy One of God" and "the Christ, the Son of the Living God." The other readings can be seen as derived from these two. "The Holy One of God" is supported by the total weight of the major Alexandrian witnesses, plus the Greek representative of the Western family. Although p^{66} includes "the Christ," it also gives evidence of the reading "the Holy One of God." The other reading is supported by the balance of the Western text and the Caesarean and Byzantine families. External evidence supports the reading "the Holy One of God." Internal evidence is even stronger in support of this reading, since it best explains the origin of the other readings. The reading of p^{66} is clearly dependent upon it. The other readings were probably borrowed from Matthew 16:16 where a similar confession of Peter is recorded in the words: "the Christ, the Son of the living God." The more difficult reading is "the Holy One of God." It is not a common title for Jesus, whereas the titles "Christ" and "Son of God." are quite common throughout the New Testament. It appears certain that "the Holy One of God" was original to the text of John.

John 7:8 reads: "Go ye up unto this feast: I go not up yet unto this feast; for my time is not yet full come" (KJV). However, another translation is: "Go up to the feast yourselves; I do not go up to this feast because My time has not yet fully come" (NASB). The basic difference is between "not yet" and "not." The difference between the terms was slight in Greek, *oupō*, and *ouk*. The reading "not" is found in: Alexandrian—Aleph, 1241, Coptic manuscripts; Western—D, the Latin tradition, Old Syriac; Byzantine—K, Pi. "Not yet" is read by: Alexandrian—p[66], p[75], B, L, T, W, X, 892, most of the Coptic; Caesarean—Theta, family 1, family 13, 700; Western—two Old Latin manuscripts; Byzantine—Delta, Psi, most minuscules, later Syriac manuscripts.

Once more we find the Alexandrian family divided, Aleph against B. Most of the Western text supports "not." All of the Caesarean and Byzantine support "not yet." External evidence cannot give us a final answer. Internal evidence supports "not." This reading best explains the origin of the other reading, mainly on the basis of being the more difficult reading. As we read the account in John, we discover that Jesus did indeed go to the feast. This must have bothered some scribes. How was it that Jesus said he was not going to the feast and yet did go? The words "not yet" appear two other times in the immediate context, verse 6 and later in verse 8. It would have been easy for the scribe to feel this must have been the correct reading and to insert it at this point. There certainly would have been no inclination on his part to change "not yet" to "not." If "not yet" was original, the change must have been by accident. However, it appears that the weight of evidence is for the reading "not."

One final passage in John must be noted. In comparing the King James Version with modern translations, it will be discovered that most modern translations place John 7:53–8:11 in a footnote or brackets or otherwise note that many ancient authorities omit these verses. The passage is omitted by: Alexandrian—p[66], p[75], Aleph, B, C, L, T, W, X, 33, 1241, some Coptic manuscripts; Caesarean—Theta, 565; Western—Old Latin, Old Syriac; Byzantine—A, N, Delta, Psi, a number of minuscules. The passage is included in: Alexandrian—892, some Coptic manuscripts; Caesarean—700; Western—D, many Old Latin manuscripts, Vulgate; Byzantine—F, G, H, K, M, U. most minuscules, later Syriac manuscripts. Some manuscripts include the passage but indicate by markings that there is question about it. The passage is included following John 21:25 by family 1 (Caesarean). It is placed after Luke 21:38 by family 13 (Caesarean). One minuscule manuscript places it after John 7:36 and another following Luke 24:53.

Once more the Alexandrian family is united in its support of the omission of this material. It is joined by the uncial representative from the Caesarean family. The Western text is also represented by the Old Syriac and some of the Old Latin. The inclusion finds support from the Greek representative of the Western text and from the Byzantine text. The Caesarean family is badly split. Theta omits it; family 1 places it after John 21:25; family 13 places it in Luke. This variation indicates that it was not part of the text in the earliest Caesarean tradition. Thus, external evidence strongly weighs against the passage being part of the original text of John. The principle of the shorter reading being preferred clearly supports omission. It is easier to see why it might have been added than why it would have been omitted. There is nothing in the passage that seemingly would have bothered any scribe. Thus, the overwhelming evidence is that the passage did not constitute part of the original text of this Gospel. However, we should note that there is no reason to doubt that it is a true story about Jesus. It sounds too much like him, and too little like anyone else, to question this fact. It is not the kind of story that the early church would have made up about Jesus, and it was undoubtedly part of the oral tradition which circulated in great volume in the early years. It became imbedded at different points in the written Gospels.

Readings from Acts

In Acts we will note only two textual problems. The first is 11:20. Some of the people who were driven from Jerusalem went to Antioch and "spake unto the Grecians" (KJV). Another reading is that they "spoke to the Greeks also" (RSV). The same reading, "Grecians," appears in the King James Version at Acts 6:1, where there is no textual question about the reading. Other translations use "Hellenists" to translate the Greek word in chapter 6. It seems to mean Greek-speaking Jews. The reading "Grecians" or "Hellenists" is supported by: Alexandrian—B, Psi, 1241; Byzantine—corrector of D, E, P, most minuscules. "Greeks" is read by: Alexandrian—p74, A; Western—D (original); Byzantine—corrector of Aleph. The Old Latin, Syriac, and Coptic made no distinction between the two terms. Aleph reads "evangelists," which is an impossible reading at this point. Presumably it must indicate that the manuscript from which the copy was being made read "Hellenists," since the two words could have been confused by a careless scribe.

The Alexandrian family is divided on this text. While Aleph and B seem to support one reading, A (Alexandrian outside the Gospels) supports the other. The Western text gives support to the reading "Greeks." The Byzantine agrees with the majority of the Alexandrian. There is no Caesarean text outside the Gospels. External authority may tend toward the reading "Grecians," or "Hellenists," but it is not totally convincing. By accident, either reading could provide the basis from which the other reading was derived. In this instance, the outlook of the scribe would determine which is the more difficult reading. Since the term "Hellenists" appears elsewhere in Acts, it would not have bothered the scribe. Intrinsic evidence is of importance in this case. One must ask what Luke was doing in the writing of his book. It appears that during these chapters he was showing how the gospel moved in steady stages from Jerusalem into other parts of the world. He had already recorded the preaching of the gospel to Samaritans, to a proselyte (at least in spirit), and to a "God-fearer." There were already Hellenists in the church (Acts 6:1). For these men in Antioch to preach to Greek-speaking Jews would have been no advancement in the gospel. Acts 11:19 has already shown that the gospel was being preached to Jews in Antioch. Thus, from Luke's perspective the reading "Greeks" must have been required. While intrinsic evidence cannot ordinarily bear such weight, it appears that here it must be the decisive factor.

The other passage in Acts to be examined is 8:37: "And Philip said, If thou believest with all thine heart, thou mayest. And he answered and said, I believe that Jesus Christ is the Son of God" (KJV). A check with recent translations shows that this verse is omitted in them, although it is included in the King James Version. The verse is omitted by: Alexandrian—p^{45}, p^{74}, Aleph, A, B, C, Psi, 33, 1241, Coptic manuscripts; Byzantine—P, three other uncials, a large number of minuscules, Syriac manuscripts. It is added by: Western—E, the Old Latin; Byzantine—a number of minuscules.

In this case, the Western is really the only family to show strong support for the inclusion of the verse. Therefore, the manuscript evidence is strongly in favor of omission. Internal evidence supports this position. It is the shorter reading, and there is no reason why a scribe would want to omit it. On the contrary, its theology would have met strong approval from the early church. If a scribe knew of the words, he would have wanted to put them in his text. This is one of many additions that the Western text makes in Acts.

Readings from Paul's Letters

We now turn to readings in Paul's writings, for example, "Therefore being justified by faith, we have peace with God through our Lord Jesus Christ" (Romans 5:1, KJV)—". . . let us continue at peace" (NEB). It is true that few translations adopt the position shown in the *New English Bible*. In fact, the standard Greek texts of today place in the text the reading which lies behind the King James Version. The difference is between two forms of the verb. One is the indicative, *echomen,* which is translated "we have." The other is the subjunctive, *echōmen,* translated "let us continue." Note that the only difference between the two forms is whether the middle vowel is long or short. The manuscript evidence for the indicative (KJV) is: Alexandrian—Psi, 1241, Coptic manuscripts; Western—G, minority of the Old Latin; Byzantine—a corrector of Aleph, a corrector of B, P, one other uncial, most minuscules, part of the Syriac. The support for the subjunctive (NEB) is: Alexandrian—Aleph (original), A, B (original),

C, 33, some Coptic manuscripts; Western—D, the majority of the Old Latin, Vulgate; Byzantine—K, a number of minuscules, Syriac manuscripts.

We see that the Alexandrian family strongly supports the subjunctive. The Western family is divided—with one important Greek manuscript on each side. The Byzantine is also divided. External evidence strongly supports the subjunctive form. When we turn to internal evidence, we realize that either reading could explain the origin of the other. In fact, it is quite likely that the change was accidental, since the two words would have been pronounced exactly the same. Yet, we should also notice that a scribe might consider the subjunctive as the more difficult reading. He might look at it and think that Paul could not be exhorting. Since peace is an actual gift from God, Paul would not suggest that we are to try to gain it, as many would translate the subjunctive, "let us have." However, since this is a present tense, it would seem that a better translation would be "let us go on having," or "let us continue." The decision to put the indicative into the text has been made by editors on the basis of intrinsic evidence, as they do not believe the subjunctive fits the context of what Paul could have written. However, with the translation suggested, it does fit the context. Since this is true—and with the very great textual support—the subjunctive is the reading which should be placed in the text. (This reminds us that we are not to be slaves to the decisions that editors make. There are times when they are probably wrong in the readings they put in the text. This is one such example.)

Colossians 2:2 gives a great variety of readings. ". . . to the acknowledgement of the mystery of God, and of the Father, and of Christ" (KJV)—". . . the knowledge of God's mystery, of Christ" (RSV). In brief form, the external evidence follows. "Of God, Christ" is read in: Alexandrian—p46, B. "Of God" is found in: Alexandrian—H, P, Coptic manuscripts; Byzantine—a corrector of D. "Of Christ" is in: Byzantine—a few minuscules. "Of God and Christ" is found in one lectionary. "Of God, which is Christ" is in D (original) and some Old Latin (all Western). "Of

God who is in Christ" is in 33 (Alexandrian). "Of God the Father in Christ Jesus" is the reading of the Armenian version (Alexandrian or Western). "Of God the Father of Christ" is read in: Alexandrian—Aleph (original), A, C, Coptic manuscripts; Western—some Old Latin, Vulgate. "Of God the Father and of Christ" is in: Western—two Vulgate manuscripts; Byzantine—one uncial manuscript, one minuscule. "Of God, even the Father of Christ" is in: Alexandrian—Psi; Byzantine—a corrector of Aleph, some minuscules, Syriac. "Of God and of the Father and of Christ" is supported by a corrector of D, K, most minuscules, Syriac (all Byzantine).

In this case, there is strong Alexandrian support for the first reading. The other readings each receive minor support, and there is no strong family support for any single one of them. Thus, external evidence leans toward the reading "of God, Christ." This reading also best explains the origin of the others. Each of the others seems to be an effort to give meaning to the very abbreviated expression "of God, Christ." Sometimes this was shortened by the omission either of God or Christ. More frequently, it was lengthened as effort was made to explain exactly what Paul meant by the phrase. However, all these explanations should be rejected as scribal efforts, and the first reading listed, the reading of p[46] and B, should be accepted as what Paul wrote.

Consider also: "God was manifest in the flesh" in 1 Timothy 3:16 (kjv). Recent translations read "He" rather than "God." Did Paul originally write "God" or "He"? "Who" (translated "He" in most translations) is read in: Alexandrian—Aleph (original), A (original), C (original), 33; Western—G; Byzantine—a few minuscules and part of the Syriac. "Which" is found in: Western—D (original), Old Latin, Vulgate. Most of the Syriac and Coptic manuscripts do not distinguish between "who" and "which." "God" is read in: Alexandrian—L, P, Psi, 1241; Byzantine—a corrector of Aleph, a corrector of A, a corrector of C, a corrector of D, K, most minuscules.

Here we discover that the Alexandrian text reads "who" and the Western text reads "which." The Byzantine reads "God."

Manuscript evidence supports the reading "who." Which reading best explains the origin of the others? "Who" agrees grammatically with an understood "Christ" in the context of the Christian hymn being quoted. Since there is no noun for "Christ" in the verse, a scribe may have thought that the reference was back to the word "mystery," and so he changed the reading to "which." There is close similarity in writing between the words for "who" and "God" (*os* and *ths*), when "God" is abbreviated. Since the capital letters *omicron* and *theta* look very much alike, confusion could have arisen by accident. No manuscript earlier than the eighth century supports the reading "God." Thus, all the evidence points to "who" as being the original reading.

Summary

We have now explored a number of variant readings in different New Testament writings. It is hoped that this has enabled the reader to see that the practice of textual criticism is more of a science than might appear on the surface. Decisions are not made simply because of the arbitrary preference of the editor of a text. Instead, evidence is evaluated and reasons are sought to explain the differences in manuscripts. On the basis of solid study and honest concern for the truth, decisions are made, usually with a great deal of confidence. And even where some uncertainty still exists as to which was the original reading, we can be grateful that these differences do not in any way affect our understanding of how God was at work, providing for our redemption in Jesus Christ. Our New Testament stands intact, and no matter what English translation one may prefer to use, we find in it God's message to us and to our world. This study should have made us less fearful and more understanding of the differences which exist between translations. In the final chapter of this book, we will explore the history of the translation of the New Testament into English. Before that, however, attention must be given to why these particular books have come to make up our New Testament.

6

Early Development of the New Testament Canon

Now that we have considered the efforts that have been expended in seeking to determine the original text of the New Testament writings, we face another question. How is it that we have these particular writings in our New Testament? Other gospels and letters were written in that early period, many of which have perished with the passage of time. Others have been preserved, and some of these may well have been written as early as some of the materials that we cherish as Scripture. Why were those writings excluded? What criteria were used by the early Christians in selecting the books which were considered authoritative? To what extent did God lead in the selection of these writings, which we call the canon?

We refer to the canon of the Old Testament and the canon of the New Testament. The Greek word, *Kanōn,* literally means a reed. It was a tool used by a carpenter or builder, and thus referred to a straight rod or bar. The term gradually came to signify written laws which serve as rules of behavior. Later, it came to mean a list or catalogue, which is close to our usage of the term.[1] Since a canon "was the general rule of doctrine or practice, the Scriptures that were generally recognized by the Church could be described as 'canonical' or 'canonized.' "[2] Thus, a canon is a list of writings considered to be God's revelation to his people and which serves as the authority for their faith and practice. The first usage of the term to refer to a list of New Testament writings was in the fourth century. Since that time, it has been commonly used in this way. Our interest in the next two chapters is to explore the gradual process by which certain writings were collected and used—up to the point where they, and they alone, were recognized and accepted as the inspired and authoritative Scriptures for Christians.

Christian Use of the Old Testament

The early Christians were in the unique position of having a book of authoritative writings from the very beginning of their existence as a separate group. Perhaps they were the only group for which this has been true at the beginning of their religious experience. They had what we know as the Old Testament, the Scriptures of the Jewish faith. Those in Palestine had these writings in the Hebrew language, while those who lived elsewhere had the Greek translation of these writings, the Septuagint. It is quite likely that the Christians inherited or adopted a group of Scriptures, not a canon. From all that we can determine, an official canon of the Old Testament was not adopted until the last part of the first century or the beginning of the second. However, for the most part, the Old Testament as we know it today was firmly established by custom in the time of Jesus.

It is traditional to divide the Old Testament into three parts: the Law, the Prophets, and the Writings. Although some Jewish tradition claims that the canon of the entire Old Testament was fixed at one time, long before the time of Jesus, this is not likely to be so. All indications are that the Law was firmly fixed by the time of Ezra, 400 B.C. We can speak of its being canonical or authoritative by that time. The Prophets (the historical books were known as "the earlier prophets" and the prophetic books were "the later prophets") were probably recognized as canon by about 200 B.C. The final determination of the Old Testament canon was not settled officially until the end of the first Christian century.

The early Christians certainly looked upon these books as their authority. They were considered the revelation of God and inspired by his Spirit, and the early believers did not seem to have any intention of replacing them or adding to them. In this they were certainly following the pattern of Jesus himself. There are clear indications in the Gospels that Jesus saw the Old Testament as God's revelation and as authoritative. He accepted the traditional ideas of authorship (Mark 12:26, 36), and he made his appeals to the written word, in contrast to the oral tradition that had been built up through the centuries. He claimed that Scripture could not be broken (John 10:35). At the same time, Jesus was willing to go behind the Scriptures to the original intention of God (Mark 10:2–12). He also showed that basic human needs are to receive priority over specific legal demands (Mark 2:25–28). Paul also made much use of the Old Testament and there is no question that he looked upon it as authority. John seldom quoted from the Old Testament, but there are constant allusions to it throughout his writings. There are specific statements in some of the New Testament writings about the inspiration of Scripture (2 Tim. 3:16; 2 Peter 1:20 f.). The writers of these claims must have been thinking of the Jewish Scriptures, the Old Testament, although we have every right to apply the claim to both Testaments. In contrast, there are very few allusions to any noncanonical writings in the New Testament. The letter of Jude is the only writing to make specific reference to such materials (vv. 9, 14). The early Christians had a scriptural authority—it was the writings of the Old Testament.

A New Authority

But there was something quite distinctive about Christianity, something which separated it from its parent religion. This, of course, was the person of Jesus. His authority was recognized even during his earthly ministry: ". . . the crowds were astonished at his teaching, for he taught them as one who had authority, and not as their scribes" (Matt. 7:28–29, RSV). A scribe had no independent authority. He could quote the Old Testament, or he could quote a rabbi from a previous generation, but he did not dare formulate any new teaching. In contrast, Jesus taught with an authority which must have come from God. His use of "truly" or "truly, truly" ("verily, verily," KJV) to introduce a statement was previously unheard of. Usually this word was the response of others to a statement. It gave assent and affirmed agreement. For Jesus to use it as an introduction to a statement was in some way a claim to divine authority. Throughout John's Gospel, we see Jesus claiming that his teaching had been given to him by the Father. Following the resurrection, he claimed, "All authority in heaven and on earth has been given to me" (Matt. 28:18, RSV).

It seems clear from the remainder of the New Testament that the authority of Jesus was recognized by his followers. In reality, he constituted an authority greater than that of the Law and the Prophets of the Old Testament. This is seen clearly in the contrasts set forth in Matthew 5:21–48. Jesus cited statements that were commonly accepted by the people, usually derived from the Old Testament. And then he set in contrast his new teaching. The early church accepted this aspect of the authority of Jesus. While it is true that Paul seldom referred directly to a teaching of Jesus, he did show that he respected the authority of Jesus. In discussing the question of marriage, he carefully distinguished between what Jesus said and what he, Paul, had to say (1 Cor. 7:10, 12). This importance attached to the words of Jesus did not come from the fact that they were written words, for probably at this time none of the Gospels had yet been written. The words had meaning and authority because they came from Jesus himself.

Thus the Christians had two authorities: the Scripture and Jesus. Of course, during this time, the words of Jesus were in oral form, suggesting that they might vary somewhat in detail in different places. Little firm control could have been exercised over the tradition. It gradually became clear that the words must be put in writing. This was especially evident when the gospel began to spread beyond the Jewish community into a Gentile world. There was danger that the truth of the gospel might be lost among people who did not have the cultural background and the emphasis on memorizing that prevailed among the Jews. This, along with other motivations, led to the writing of Gospels during the last half of the first century. These Gospels contained the words of Jesus as well as his acts, and these recorded words must have been accepted as authoritative from the very first. However, we must realize that this did not eliminate the passing on of Jesus' teaching in oral form. Even in the middle of the second century, there were those who claimed to prefer the oral tradition of the living voice to written records of Jesus.

Alongside these two authorities, a third arose, that of the "Apostles." Evidently great emphasis was placed upon the apostles, the companions of Jesus during his ministry and considered the official interpreters of the Lord. In a sense, this meant that if one rejected the apostles, he was at the same time rejecting Jesus. (It may be that the division of Law and Prophets in the Old Testament prepared the way for the twofold division of Gospel and Apostles in what was to become the New Testament.) It was obviously necessary that the teaching of Jesus be interpreted and applied. No one could claim the right to do this to any greater degree than those who had been with him during his ministry, or who had been called in a special way such as Paul. By the early second century, these men were considered to be a group that could not be contradicted. The apostles were present in their writings, for the most part letters. Thus, there are thirteen letters in the New Testament attributed to one man, Paul. And these men would have an authority only slightly below that of Jesus himself, for it was believed that they taught and wrote with the inspiration of the Spirit of God (1 Cor. 7:40).

The Earliest Use of Christian Writings

It must be remembered that in these early years, no Christian had any idea of adding materials to the Scripture, the Old Testament. Evidently Jesus had written nothing, and there is no apparent command from him that his followers write anything. It seems that even the Gospels were not originally intended to be placed on a level with the Old Testament. Paul's writings were occasional, that is, directed to a particular problem in the church to which the letter was addressed. There is no indication that he thought these writings might be preserved and classed as Scripture. In fact, the only writing in the New Testament that gives such an impression is the Book of Revelation (22:18 f.).

> The books of the New Testament were written one and all by members of the earliest Christian communities to meet particular situations and emergencies which arose within those communities. They were in origin neither Scripture nor Literature, but the natural and inevitable product of the growing infant Church.[3]

Although it is true that the Gospels contained the authoritative words of Jesus, this did not mean that the books themselves were, at first, considered authoritative, or Scripture. While Paul's writings were recognized as valuable, especially by the churches to which they were originally addressed, no one thought of placing them on an equality with the Old Testament. Such elevation was to require the passing of many years. Writings needed to be highly prized over a wide area for a long period of time before they could achieve a status comparable to the Old Testament. B. F. Westcott pointed out that only time brought a change in the situation of the church regarding its writings.

> As soon as the immediate disciples of the Apostles had passed away, it was felt that the tradition of the Apostolic teaching had lost its direct authority. Heretics arose who claimed to be possessed of other traditionary rules derived in succession from St Peter or St Paul, and it was only possible to try their authenticity by documents beyond the reach of change or corruption. Dissensions arose within the Church itself, and the appeal to the written word of the Apostles became natural and decisive. And thus the practical belief of the primitive age was first definitely expressed when the Church had gained a permanent position, and a fixed literature.[4]

There is every reason to believe that all, or almost all, of our New Testament books were written before the end of the first century. Unfortunately, there are few other Christian writings from the first century which help us to understand how these writings were considered by churches or individuals. The only such writing which can be placed definitely within the first century is the letter from Clement, bishop of Rome, to the church at Corinth. This letter, known as 1 Clement, is usually dated A.D. 95. Although this lack of evidence makes it only a theory, it is likely that the collection of Paul's letters began in the last decade of the first century.

R. M. Grant states: ". . . toward the end of the first century a collection of Pauline letters was in existence, though we do not know that such a collection was universally accepted or that there were not various collections in existence."[5] One does not need to accept the elaborate theories of E. J. Goodspeed[6] and John Knox[7] to agree that this compilation took place. Both of these men believed that the collection was made by a man who knew Paul and possessed two of his letters, Colossians and Philemon.

With the publication of Acts, the man discovered that Paul had founded other churches. He decided to investigate whether any of these churches had received and preserved letters from Paul. And he discovered that letters were kept in Rome, Corinth, Thessalonica, Philippi, and Galatia. According to this theory, the man then composed Ephesians to serve as an introduction to the collection of letters. The suggestion is even made that the collector was Onesimus, the slave of Philemon, who later may have become bishop of Ephesus. This makes an interesting story, but there is no way to determine whether there is any truth in it.

Nevertheless, it is indeed likely that Paul's letters were collected about this date. The climate was right for it, and they would prove quite helpful in settling disputes that were arising over doctrinal matters, since the note of authority in them would be of great value. At least some of Paul's letters were known at the time of the writing of 2 Peter (3:15–16). The big argument for the collection of the letters at this time is that early in the second century, writers seem to have known a number of these letters. In a sense, Paul himself gave the impetus to the collection of his letters when he encouraged the church at Colossae: "And when this letter has been read among you, have it read also in the church of the Laodiceans; and see that you read also the letter from Laodicea" (Col. 4:16, RSV). W. Barclay argues that it was in Ephesus that Paul's letters were first collected.

> It was there that Paul spent three years, longer than in any other place in the days of his freedom. It was there that Revelation with its seven letters was published; it was there that the Johnannine letters with their knowledge of Paul were published; it was in Asia Minor that the Ignatian collection was made; and it is there that references to the letters of Paul as a collection appear.[8]

Mention has already been made of 1 Clement. The writer of this letter was quite well aware of certain of our New Testament writings. It is almost certain that he made use of Romans, 1 Corinthians, and Hebrews in his letter to Corinth. Grant[9] points out that there are more than a dozen definite allusions to 1 Corinthians in this letter, as well as a specific reference to "the epistle of the blessed Paul the apostle." He notes eleven allusions to Romans, one of them being a paraphrase of Romans 1:29–32. The allusions to Hebrews are quite certain, although Clement does not mention a title or author of the work. In addition, Grant claims that Clement was familiar with Galatians, Philippians, Ephesians, and probably James and 1 Peter.

At this point, a word of caution must be inserted. It appears that many writers on the development of the New Testament canon are extremely free in stating that certain Christian writers knew or made use of certain New Testament books. Often the evidence is not sufficient to support the position that is stated. It must take more than the use of one or two words, unusual as those may be, to indicate use of a particular writing. The studies of this author, along with that of students in classes and seminars, have suggested that there is far less certainty than is often indicated about the use of New Testament writings by these early Christians. It seems best to state only that which is certain, although this may mean that references to some books of the New Testament will not be found until fairly late in the development of the canon.

There is no clear evidence that Clement was familiar with any of our Gospels. He did know of teachings of Jesus, but it seems that he must have derived these from either oral sources or writings other than the New Testament Gospels. Because his use of Christian materials is so different from the way in which he cites the Old Testament, it is clear that Clement did not regard the Christian writings as Scripture. Although they were authoritative, they were not considered in the same light as was the Old Testament.

A second writer of this period was Ignatius (bishop of Antioch early in the second century and martyred in Rome, A.D. 115). Seven of his letters, written about A.D. 115, have been preserved. In these we find frequent use of Christian writings, especially the letters of Paul. While direct quotations are few, it appears that Ignatius may have known as many as eight of Paul's letters (Romans, 1 Corinthians, Galatians, Ephesians, Philippians, Colossians, 1 Thessalonians, and 2 Thessalonians). It is also possible that he was familiar with 1 Peter as well. There is disagreement as to what knowledge he may have had of written gospels since, again, there are no direct quotations. Scholars differ drastically in their evaluation of "allusions" to the Gospels. It may be safe to suggest that, in the absence of any direct quotations, Ignatius may have made use of oral materials rather than of written Gospels.

The next writing of this period is the letter of Polycarp, the bishop of Smyrna, who was martyred about A.D. 155. The claim was made—and there is no reason to doubt it—that Polycarp was acquainted with some of the apostles of Jesus, especially John. Polycarp wrote a letter to the church at Philippi, although there is disagreement as to the date which should be assigned to this letter. Some authorities would date it "early," that is, while Ignatius was still living, while others place it shortly before Polycarp's death. Polycarp, too, knew a number of Paul's letters. He mentions "letters" which Paul had written to Philippi, although it is uncertain whether he meant more than one letter. If he did, was he making reference to the letters to Thessalonica as being written to Philippi?

Or did he know of another letter to Philippi which has since disappeared?

It seems likely that Polycarp had a collection of letters greatly similar to that with which Ignatius was familiar. In addition, it is possible that in his writing we have the earliest allusions to 1 Timothy and 2 Timothy. Polycarp may also have known the Gospel of Matthew. Surprisingly, in the light of his probable acquaintance with the apostle John, there is nothing in his letter to suggest any knowledge of the Gospel of John. We should remember that in neither Ignatius nor Polycarp is there any suggestion that these Christian writings were considered Scripture. They were valuable, but were not yet considered on a level with the Old Testament.

The Epistle of Barnabas has been dated from as early as the late first century to as late as the middle of the second century, although it was probably written early in the second century. We have no knowledge of its author. There is no reason to suppose that it was written by the Barnabas of Acts who was Paul's companion. This is the first writing to introduce a quotation, seemingly from one of the Gospels, with the expression "it is written," which was the common way of introducing quotations from the Old Testament. Barnabas quotes Matthew 22:14, "Many are called but few are chosen." This does seem to indicate that Matthew was already known, which should not be surprising at all. However, it has been pointed out that the author had a very loose concept of Scripture. He would include such a writing as the apocalyptic book of 1 Enoch as part of the Old Testament Scripture. Thus, his use of Matthew does not tell us much about the authority that was given to the book at this early date.

Two other books from this early period must be noted. One is The Teaching of the Twelve Apostles, better known as the Didache and usually dated in the early part of the second century. In this writing, we find the statement, "As the Lord commanded in his Gospel" (8:2). Later (9:5), there is a quotation of a statement found in Matthew 7:6, "Do not give the holy thing to the dogs." However, it is not clear whether these references are to a written Gospel. It is entirely possible that the writer was dependent upon oral tradition. If he was relying upon a written document, it was probably the Gospel of Matthew. However, the writer was not interested in books as such. For him, it was important that it was tradition, whether oral or written. Thus, although he may have known and used the Gospel of Matthew, it was not Scripture for him.

Another early book is the Shepherd of Hermas, written by Hermas from Rome, probably early in the second century. The allusions to Christian writings in this work are not so clear as in the Didache. Certainly this writer made reference to no writings different from the ones we have already noted as being alluded to by others in this period. And he did not look upon any of them as Scripture.

It must have become evident to the reader that it is extremely difficult to feel on firm ground in this earliest period of writings. The fact that the writers did not claim to be making direct quotations, along with the recognition that they were using language which must have been quite common among Christians, makes one hesitant to reach firm conclusions about the actual use of New Testament materials. There is much subjectivity in deciding whether a particular phrase is a true allusion to a certain New Testament work, since it might just as easily be understood as a phrase borrowed from the common preaching and teaching of the day. Conclusions are often based on the presuppositions of the student of the materials. However, lest that disturb us too much, we are not concerned in this study with the point in time when a particular book of the New Testament was first known or used. What is important is when that book was first elevated to a position of authority equal to or superior to the Old Testament.[10] In other words, our concern is with the time when a writing achieved canonical status. There is general agreement that no books reached this pinnacle during the first period, up to A.D. 140.

> We take our stand, then, at the beginning of the second century, and during, roughly, the first three-quarters of it we find the conception of a canon being formed, i.e. the separa-

tion of a group of apostolic writings from all other Christian writings to be reverenced on a level with the Old Testament.[11]

H. von Campenhausen points out: "In the first one and a half centuries of the Church's history there is no single Gospel writing which is directly made known, named, or in any way given prominence by quotation."[12]

The First Formation of a New Testament Canon

Matters become somewhat clearer when we come to the time of Marcion. This man plays an important role in the development of a New Testament canon, although there is some disagreement as to how much credit should be given to him for inaugurating the idea of a fixed collection of books. Marcion was born in Sinope in Pontus (Asia Minor) and was the son of a bishop. Later he went to Rome, where some of his ideas were branded as heretical. This was probably about A.D. 140. He had a great deal of trouble with the ethical issues in the Old Testament, and finally he came to the position where he rejected all of the Old Testament writings. Marcion claimed that the God of the Old Testament could not be the same being as the God and Father of the Lord Jesus Christ. The God of Jesus showed himself as a loving and merciful God, while the Old Testament figure was sometimes immoral. Of course, Marcion was not the only one in the middle of the second century who rejected the Old Testament as having no authority for Christians. But our interest in him is not entirely in the matter of his attitude toward the Old Testament. Rather, he drew up a list of Christian writings for the use of his followers, and it is the first list of authoritative Christian writings of which there is any record.

Marcion's canon, if we may call it such, is significant in what it contained, as well as in what does not appear in it. He included one Gospel, Luke. It would be more accurate to say that he had the Gospel of Luke as it was edited by himself. This means that he omitted from it everything which seemed to put the Old Testament and the Old Testament God in a favorable light. Thus, the birth narratives in chapters 1 and 2 had to be omitted. In addition to a Gospel, Marcion also included an apostle, Paul. His list contained ten letters from Paul, apparently all of those attributed to him today with the exception of the Pastoral Epistles (1 Timothy, 2 Timothy, and Titus). But, again, these letters were edited. It is true that we do not have the actual production of Marcion's work. We are dependent upon some of his opponents, particularly Tertullian and Epiphanius, who were quite critical of him in his attempts to remove everything from these writings which did not meet his approval.

It seems clear that the canon of Marcion was a theological development. This means that he chose the books to be included on the basis of his theological assumptions. Luke's Gospel appeared to him to be the least Jewish and thus the most acceptable. We do not know how many other Gospels may have come to his attention. But with his anti-Jewish bias, Luke certainly fit his purposes best. The same thing can be said of his choice of Paul, who seemingly fit his conception of what an apostle should be. Marcion found far less that would be offensive in Paul's material than he would have found in 1 Peter, for example. Marcion opposed everything which might be termed law and every concept of righteousness grounded on a legalistic basis. While Marcion might have based his ideas on Paul, he went far beyond anything that the apostle had ever conceived. Since he was a literalist in his approach to Scripture, this is what gave him so much trouble with the Old Testament. Other Christians might take some of the material symbolically and thus have little difficulty with it. Marcion did not do this and the result was the outright rejection of the Old Testament. He also believed that the true message of Jesus had been infected with false ideas brought in by a Judaizing group within the church. Marcion saw his task as reformation, getting back to the original teaching of Jesus in its purity. For this he needed written documents. Oral tradition could not suffice. There had to be a Gospel and an apostle to whom appeal could be made to support his theology.[13]

The order in which Marcion listed Paul's letters is puzzling. His collection had them in this order: Galatians, 1 and 2 Corinthians, Romans, 1 and 2 Thessalonians, Laodiceans, Colossians, Philemon, and Philippians. It is easy to see why Galatians was first in his list, since it can easily be considered the most anti-Jewish of any of Paul's writings. Its theology would be deeply appreciated by Marcion (at least his understanding of that theology). The other letters seem to have been placed in order according to length (at least in general). This assumes that the two Corinthian letters would be considered as one item and the two to Thessalonica in the same way. It is generally agreed that the letter listed as Laodiceans is the New Testament's Ephesians. There is no indication that Marcion had any manuscript which entitled the letter in this way. It was probably a guess based upon the reference in Colossians 4:16.

There has been much discussion about the canon of Marcion. Was it the first one to be formed? Or did he take a previously formed canon and remove some of the materials from it to form his own? Since this is a matter of continued discussion, there is no proof either way. However, there is no historical evidence of such a collection and listing of writings prior to the time of Marcion. Therefore, it seems best to assume that he was the first one to make such a list. Perhaps he was the first one whose theology demanded that a list be available. We assume that he was familiar with other Gospels, but we cannot know which ones. It has often been stated that he rejected the Pastoral Epistles, but once more, we must be cautious. There is no evidence that he rejected them. Although it is true that he might not have appreciated some of the material in them, it is safer to say simply that he did not include them in his canon. It is possible that he was not aware of them.

The activity of Marcion presented the church with a dilemma. It could not leave the situation as it found it at this time. The heresy of Marcion must be opposed, and appeal must be made to written materials to support the position of the main body of the church. They could reject the writings that Marcion had included in his canon, or they could accept those writings and add to them others which were used and appreciated by the larger church. We see that it was the latter approach that was followed.

First, the church affirmed the Old Testament. It did not surrender it because of Marcion and others who refused to admit its inspiration and authority.

Second, it admitted that Marcion had one Gospel. But the church claimed more than one, and by the end of the second century the number will have become fixed at four. Thus, Marcion had only a part of the truth. In fact, his one Gospel was mutilated. This gave the church a basis for refuting Marcion's theology.

The same thing happened with regard to the letters. Marcion might claim one apostle, Paul. The church accepted him as well, but it also claimed at least two more, Peter and John—because by this time 1 Peter and 1 John seem to have been widely known and accepted. So it seems that the action of Marcion gave great impetus to the formation of a New Testament canon. Certainly, the books would have been brought together sooner or later. But the process was hastened by the heresies which the church had to combat, and progress was rapid during the remainder of the second century.

7

Final Determination of the New Testament Canon

As we reach the middle of the second century, we discover that the use of Christian writings became more widespread and references more specific. In fact, it appears that the basic nucleus of a New Testament canon was generally agreed upon by the close of that century.

Witnesses from the Middle of the Second Century

The first writing to designate clearly a collection of Jesus' sayings as Scripture—and as on an equality with the Old Testament—was the writing known as 2 Clement. This writing, a sermon written about the middle of the second century, has no relation to the letter of 1 Clement. After a quotation from Isaiah, the writer then states: "Another scripture also says," and then he quotes Matthew 9:13, "I come not to call the righteous but sinners."[1] The significant thing here is that the writing which contained the words of Jesus now seems to have been viewed as Scripture. While all along the words of Jesus had been considered authoritative, it is only now that the *writings* which contained those words were raised to a similar position of authority. Of course, this was the logical and almost inevitable outcome of the view that Jesus' words had authority. The position of 2 Clement with regard to other New Testament writings is not so clear. It is likely that the author had, and made use of, some of Paul's letters, but it is not clear whether they had the same scriptural status as the Gospel of Matthew.

The key figure in this period is Justin Martyr. Since he died about A.D. 165, his writings cover the period beginning about A.D. 150. His main works were a *Dialogue* with Trypho and two *Apologies*. Justin was a Greek Samaritan, had received training in the Greek philosophical schools, and was converted at Ephesus. He used a combination of Greek philosophy and rabbinical logic in an effort to show that Jesus was truly the fulfillment of the messianic prophecies of the Old Testament. In these writings, he referred to "our Scriptures." This must mean that he was thinking of a fairly well defined group of writings which were different from the writings accepted and used by the Jews. It appears that Justin was most interested in Gospels, and he stated that the first act of worship in the Christian assemblies was to read from the Memoirs of the Apostles or from the prophets. These Memoirs certainly were Gospels. Evidently Justin accepted the idea that they were written by apostles, or perhaps by their followers. We know that he placed these Gospels on a level with the prophetic writings of the Old Testament. It must be assumed that this attribution of scriptural authority to the Gospels represented the position of the Roman church at this point in history.

Of course, we want to know which writings Justin considered to be authoritative. It appears that he knew and accepted the Gospels of Matthew, Mark, and Luke, but his use of the Gospel of John is not so clear. It is interesting that he did not make specific use of Paul's letters in his writings. While it does not seem possible that he was unaware of these letters, perhaps he hesitated to include them because of the use to which they had been put by Marcion. The witness of Justin is quite important. Jülicher commented: "It seems to me that there is more here than a mere 'germ of the New Testament Canon' . . ."[2]

In the Eastern church at about this same time, a man named Papias wrote five books entitled *An Exposition of the Oracles of the Lord*. Unfortunately, the only remnants of these writings which remain are quotations found particularly in the writings of Eusebius from the fourth century. In the middle of the second century, Papias was bishop of Hieropolis, near Laodicea. He knew of Gospels, particularly those of Matthew and Mark. In addition, he seems to have used the "Gospel of the Hebrews." However, he did not consider any of these as Scripture. In fact, he indicated that the oral voice was of more importance than the writings which might be available. According to Eusebius, Papias also made use of the letters of 1 John and 1 Peter.

About A.D. 170 in Rome, Tatian composed his Diatessaron. As the name implies, this was an attempt to consolidate the four Gospels into one single connected account. (*Dia* means through, and *tessaron* is the number four.) Evidently Tatian used only the four canonical Gospels. It is true that he may have used oral materials in addition to the written Gospels. However, since we do not have his work in the original language, whether Greek or Syriac, it is impossible to be certain about the materials that went into its composition. Its main significance for our purposes is that it indicates that by A.D. 170 the four Gospels had reached a place of unique authority in the Roman church. While other gospels might on occasion be used in different localities, it was only these four which had been elevated to positions of authority within the church.

The Close of the Second Century

Three names stand out at the close of the second century. They represent three widely scattered sections of the church. Irenaeus was bishop of Lyons (southern France) during the last quarter of the second century. Tertullian was in Carthage, North Africa, at about the same time and continued there until his death, about A.D. 220. Clement was the head of the school in Alexandria, Egypt, during the last part of the second century. He died about A.D. 212. While these men represent different areas of the Christian world, their positions on the canon are surprisingly similar.

With Irenaeus, the fourfold character of the Gospels became fixed. In fact, for him, it was a necessity that there were four.

> For, since there are four zones of the world in which we
> live, and four principal winds, while the Church is scattered

throughout all the world, and the "pillar and ground" of the Church is the Gospel and the spirit of life; it is fitting that she should have four pillars, breathing out immortality on every side, and vivifying men afresh. From which fact, it is evident that the Word, the Artificer of all, He that sitteth upon the cherubim, and contains all things, He who was manifested to men, has given us the Gospel under four aspects, but bound together by one Spirit.[3]

We may smile as we read his argument that divine creation requires four gospels, but no question was raised from this time on with regard to the authority of these writings. However, we should not assume that this decision occurred suddenly. H. Campenhausen has pointed out that the fourfold gospel was not a conscious creation. It was formed gradually but in the end was accepted universally.[4] C. F. D. Moule stated:

> But the point is that what ultimately emerged was not a single gospel but four—neither more nor less. Marcion and Tatian both tried, in their different ways, to establish a single Gospel, but did not carry the whole Church with them. The process of selection was well under way before ever it began to be consciously reasoned about or rationalized: owing to a variety of causes . . . the four-Gospel canon slid into existence almost furtively. It was certainly not the arbitrary decision of a single Christian body, still less of an individual. Its formal declaration, when it was made, was only the recognition, by the Church collectively, of a conviction that had long been silently growing on their consciousness. Perhaps at least one or two of these writings had been regularly used in assemblies for worship long before they were officially described as authoritative.[5]

Irenaeus also included an apostle as well as a Gospel. He knew and made use of all the thirteen letters of Paul, although Philemon is never quoted. He also included 1 Peter, 1 and 2 John, Acts, and Revelation. Thus he accepted as Scripture twenty-two of our twenty-seven canonical books. He can be considered "the first man to know and acknowledge a New Testament both in theory and in practice."[6]

The witness of Tertullian is very similar. He, too, used only the four Gospels and thirteen letters of Paul. The rest of his collection differed only in that he seemingly made no reference to 2 John (this is not surprising, given the shortness of that letter), but he did include Jude. He also used Hebrews, which he knew as the Letter of Barnabas. Thus, Tertullian used twenty-three of our New Testament writings.

The situation of Clement is somewhat different, for the reason that in Alexandria the definition of canon had always been somewhat looser. Clement accepted our four Gospels, but he also occasionally used other "gospels," such as the Gospel of the Hebrews and the Gospel of the Egyptians. While he seemed to find material of value in these writings, he did recognize that they were not accepted throughout most of the church. Clement accepted and used the thirteen letters of Paul, but he also included Hebrews under the name of Paul, as had been considered true in Alexandria even before his time. Since he recognized the problem with this position, his solution was to suggest that Paul wrote the letter in Hebrew and that Luke translated it into Greek. Clement also used the other writings that were known to Irenaeus and Tertullian: Acts, 1 Peter, 1 and 2 John, Jude, and Revelation. Along with these, he considered certain other writings of value, such as 1 Clement, the Shepherd of Hermas, the Didache, and the Epistle of Barnabas (not the epistle used by Tertullian). He also referred to the Apocalypse of Peter, the Acts of Paul, and the Preaching of Peter. A few years ago, a portion of a letter was discovered that presumably was written by Clement. In this letter, he made reference to a second edition of the Gospel of Mark that was prepared in Alexandria for a select group within the church.[7] Thus, we discover that Clement's limitation of the canon was not as clear as was that of Irenaeus and Tertullian. He was willing to use many other writings that were not commonly recognized elsewhere. It required the passage of a number of years before clear limitation of the canon would be seen in Alexandria.

There is one other writing that is usually dated from about this same period of time. It is known as the Muratorian Canon. Recently the suggestion has been made that the writing does not represent the Roman church at the end of the second century, but rather the Eastern church in the fourth century.[8] However, since most scholars still place it at the end of the second century, a brief note is worthwhile here. The document was discovered in the library of Milan, Italy, in 1740 by the librarian, L. A. Muratori. It is written in very poor Latin, but is thought to be a translation of an early Greek document. The beginning of the manuscript is missing, but it clearly must refer to our four Gospels. It also lists Acts, thirteen letters of Paul, Jude, 1 and 2 John, Revelation, the Apocalypse of Peter, with the notation that "some of our body will not have it read in the Church."[9] The document states that the Wisdom of Solomon, although not written by Solomon, is acknowledged. However, the Shepherd of Hermas is not acknowledged because it was written too recently by Hermas, the brother of Pius, bishop of Rome. The strange thing about this list is not only the inclusion of the Apocalypse of Peter, but even more the omission of 1 Peter. Various attempts have been made to explain this omission, but none is truly satisfactory.

Motives for Development of a Canon

At this point, we must ask a question that the reader may already have asked. On what criteria were books accepted into the developing canon of the New Testament—and on what basis were other books rejected? The answer to this question has been noticeably missing in all of the discussion that has taken place. It is true that some writings make brief reference to these matters. For example, the Muratorian Canon indicated that the contents of the Gospels were vouched for by one or another of the apostles. It is claimed that Luke wrote from his own experience in Acts. Paul wrote seven (the perfect number) letters addressed to communities, but which have value for us? The four private letters prove to be of value for church discipline and therefore were included on that basis. Irenaeus indicated that the one essential requirement above all others was that the Gospels were based upon the trustworthy testimony of an eyewitness or one who was a disciple of an eyewitness.

In addition, the writing must have total agreement with the universally accepted tradition of the church. However, Jülicher has pointed out that ". . . it was not till men already possessed a New Testament that they began to consider why they had it in precisely that form. The Church created the new Canon *unconsciously*, not according to any principles."[10]

The very necessity of the situation demanded that the church have its own Scriptures. When the break came with the Jewish synagogue, the Christians needed writings which they could claim as their own. Furthermore, the development of heresies required an accepted list of authoritative writings which could be used in opposition to those heresies and in support of the teaching of the orthodox community.

As we look back on the process, it appears that at least three criteria were employed, although indeed it may be that they were operating without conscious thought or formulation. First, and perhaps most important, was the idea that the writing was written by an apostle or the follower of an apostle. This is seen in the attributing of the Gospels to two who were among the original followers of Jesus, and two who were closely associated with apostles. The remainder of the writings were similarly understood. As will be seen, when Hebrews was brought into the canon of the church in Rome, it could only make its way when it was thought of as having been written by Paul. We should not assume any sort of critical scholarship on the part of those who accepted these writings, nor can we know the origin of the traditions which assigned names to certain of the writings.

Second, there was the recognition that the writing must be doctrinally pure. By this time, the church had something of a standard which was accepted as being true belief. No writing could be thought of as inspired and thus as Scripture unless it was in basic agreement with this standard. This was especially true as heresies began to develop. We can understand that writings would be looked at carefully to make certain there was nothing in them which could be used by such groups to support their positions.

Third, the churches had to recognize the helpfulness of these writings. This means that over a long period of time, and throughout a large geographical area, these writings had been used to advantage by Christian communities. If a writing was helpful, it was treasured, kept, used, and shared with others.

While nothing has been said about it, we must assume that the Spirit of God was at work in the selection and preservation of these writings. While, on the surface, the process represented the spontaneous decisions of individual churches throughout the Christian world, God was active in making certain that the proper writings were chosen. This is not surprising when we accept the idea that he was also active in the writing of the materials. Surely, if he inspired the writers, he would also lead their successors in the selection of the materials to form the authoritative canon of Scripture. But it is interesting to see that God worked through individuals and their churches to accomplish this purpose. He did not hand down some divine decree from heaven, nor did he accomplish his task through the convening of some great church council. God trusted himself and his purposes to people, common people, who were willing to be led by his Spirit. And if we should turn to some of the writings which were rejected by the churches, we would be impressed by the great difference of content and spirit demonstrated in the writings accepted into the canon, in contrast to those which were rejected. We cannot question the wisdom of the people who made the decisions in those early centuries.

Developments in the Third and Fourth Centuries

As we move beyond the second century, it is best to consider the development of the canon in two areas, the Greek church and the Latin church. As noted above, the Greek churches, centered in Alexandria, were always freer in regard to the use of Christian writings than were the churches in the West. This situation continued with Origen, the successor of Clement. Origen became head of the school in Alexandria in A.D. 203 and later moved to Caesarea and founded a school there. He died in A.D. 254, and was perhaps the greatest scholar of the early church. Origen accepted the new Scriptures as equal to the old. The term *the new covenant* was a familiar one to him. As with others, Origen included four Gospels, but he made use of other gospel material less frequently than Clement had done. He accepted all of the letters of Paul, although he did question the authorship of Hebrews—he was happy to keep it in his New Testament, but he admitted that no one knew who the human author was. Origen's attitude toward the other letters, all of which were known to him, was much the same as others of his time. The letters of 1 John and 1 Peter were of great importance, but the others were probably not considered of equal value. He included the Book of Revelation, although he presumably may not have been in sympathy with it. He did make use of some writings that did not end up in the New Testament, but these were fewer in number than with Clement.

Origen did one thing that was of great value for the future of the canon. He divided writings into three categories—those universally accepted, those that were false, and those that were disputed. As might be expected, the universally accepted writings included the four Gospels, Acts, fourteen letters of Paul (although he was aware that the Western church did not accept Hebrews), 1 John, 1 Peter, and Revelation. The doubtful books were 2 Peter, 2 and 3 John, James, Jude, the Shepherd of Hermas, the Didache, the Epistle of Barnabas, and the Gospel of the Hebrews. A number of writings were included in the false category, most of which were never considered authoritative at any time in any large segment of the church. The influence of Origen was great, and his practice of listing the books was followed by the other significant man in the Eastern church, Eusebius.

Eusebius wrote a history of the church about A.D. 325, and we are dependent upon him for many of the materials from an earlier age which he copied in his history. However, our interest centers in his references to the books of the New Testament. Like Origen, Eusebius divided the writings into different categories, and his list of accepted books was identical with that of his predecessor. His list of disputed books was slightly different. It included James, Jude, 2 Peter, 2 and 3 John, Barnabas, the Didache, and the Gospel of the Hebrews. But it also included the Acts of Paul, the

Apocalypse of Peter, and surprisingly, Revelation. Eusebius included Revelation in both lists! This indicates something of the situation in the Eastern church following A.D. 200. More will be said about this in the discussion of the history of individual writings.

It will be seen that a consensus was being reached in the Eastern church with regard to a canon. The only question that remained was what to do with the doubtful books. Since that category could not be kept, the books must either migrate upward into the canon or drop out of use altogether. This is what took place within the next fifty years.

A word should be said at this point about the canon of the Syriac church, which reflects a great reluctance to include writings, especially letters. For many years, its Gospel was the Diatessaron of Tatian. Later, the Gospel of "the Separated Ones" made its way into the canon. The General Epistles and Revelation do not seem to have formed a part of the canon of that church until after the fourth century.

The Latin church, centered in Rome, also showed a greater reluctance to include writings than was true in Alexandria. Hippolytus (died about A.D. 220) had a canon of about twenty-two or twenty-four books, which did not include James, Jude, and 3 John. He did not consider that Paul wrote Hebrews, which placed its status in doubt, and he did not seem to look upon 2 Peter as Scripture.

Cyprian was a successor of Tertullian in North Africa, and his New Testament was greatly similar to that of Tertullian. However, he does not seem to have made use of Hebrews. Of the General Epistles, he had only 1 Peter and 1 John.

Codex Claromotanus contains a list of Christian writings. While the manuscript is from the sixth century, it is believed that the list goes back to the fourth century and may represent the situation in Rome in the early part of that century. This list includes the four Gospels, ten letters of Paul (Philippians, and 1 and 2 Thessalonians are missing, perhaps by accidental omission), 1 and 2 Peter, James, 1, 2, and 3 John, Jude, Revelation, and Acts. On a somewhat lower level are placed Barnabas (Hebrews?), the Shepherd of Hermas, the Acts of Paul, and the Apocalypse of Peter. This is perhaps the earliest reference to James in the Western church.

The first man to list our current twenty-seven books of the New Testament as canonical—these and no others—was Athanasius, bishop of Alexandria, in his Easter Epistle of A.D. 367. This man was deposed from his position as bishop on five occasions and each time made a journey to the West. Thus, Athanasius was quite familiar with the position of the church in Rome with regard to the New Testament writings. This undoubtedly was helpful to him in making his list. It is likely that his purpose was to exclude the many apocryphal books which were circulating. His interest to us "is that *he is the earliest to lay down the twenty-seven books of our New Testament as alone canonical.*"[11] The main effect for the church in Alexandria was the final inclusion of Revelation into the canon.

The important name in the West at this time is Jerome, who died about A.D. 420. In carrying out the commission of the pope to make a new Latin translation of the Bible, he had journeyed to the East, and in the process had learned something of the attitude toward various books in the Eastern church. One of these was especially interesting to Jerome, the letter to the Hebrews. He found it a very valuable work and was anxious that it be included in the New Testament he was preparing. Jerome was even willing to indicate that it was written by Paul, although there is reason to believe that he did not actually think this to be true. However, he was the key figure in the final fixing of the canon for the church in Rome.

It is only after all of this that the church councils began to list the canonical books of the New Testament. The Council of Laodicea, A.D. 363, in its sixtieth canon lists our twenty-seven books of the New Testament, although it is generally believed that this was a later addition to the results of that council. In A.D. 393, a council was held in Hippo in North Africa. It set forth a list of New Testament writings identical with our New Testament, and the same was true of the council held in Carthage in A.D. 397. In both

of these compilations, the letters of Paul were listed as "13 epistles of the Apostle Paul and one to the Hebrews by the same
Apostle." It is only at the next council of Carthage (A.D. 419)
where Augustine was the primary figure, that the list reads "14
letters of the Apostle Paul."

History of New Testament Books

A brief survey of the history of the various books of the New
Testament may help to clarify the story of the development of the
canon.

While the Gospels were not the earliest writings of the New
Testament, they were the earliest to be considered authoritative
and scriptural. They were known early in the second century and
by the middle of that century—in the writings of 2 Clement and
Justin Martyr—were placed on the level of the Old Testament as
Scripture. By about A.D. 130, Heracleon, a Gnostic heretic, had
written a commentary on John. After the middle of the second
century, no question seems to have been raised about any of our
Gospels. It only remained for the use of certain apocryphal "gospels" to be discontinued.

The history of the Book of Acts is not so clear. While there may
be allusions to it in earlier writings, the first man definitely to refer
to it and show its authoritative status was Irenaeus. After that time,
Acts had a fixed place in the canon. It served as a fitting introduction to the Epistles, and usually was placed immediately before
them in the manuscripts.

The earliest collection of Paul's letters probably occurred in the
late first century. By the middle of the second century, Marcion
had composed his canon, which included ten letters of Paul, all
except the Pastoral Epistles. Even earlier, Ignatius and Polycarp
showed a familiarity with a large number of Paul's writings. Clement of Rome, late in the first century, was familiar with at least two
of Paul's letters. The church did not reject Paul's writings simply
because they had been used by Marcion in his own way and to
support his own ideas. Rather, they accepted them, including the

Pastorals. Again, the key figure is Irenaeus, who quoted from all of Paul's writings, except for Philemon. It is not surprising that Irenaeus did not make use of this writing—for there was little, if anything, in it of value in his opposition to the heresies of the day. From the time of Irenaeus, Paul's writings were a clear part of the New Testament.

The letter to the Hebrews is an interesting puzzle. Clement knew of it when he wrote in A.D. 95. After that, its use ceased in the Western church with the exception of Tertullian in North Africa at the end of the second century—and Tertullian knew the letter as having been written by Barnabas rather than by Paul. Even Irenaeus did not seem to be familiar with the writing. However, in the Eastern church, the situation was quite different. From the very earliest references, we find that Hebrews was known and was accepted as having been written by Paul, although this attribution to Paul was difficult to maintain. Clement of Alexandria accepted that Paul wrote it in Hebrew, and he claimed that it was translated by Luke. Origen was willing to accept the letter and even attributed it to Paul, although he admitted that no one knew who the author was except God. However, no questions were raised in the church of Alexandria about Hebrews in so far as its place in the canon was concerned. It was not until the time of Jerome that the letter began to be accepted in the Roman church. There seems no question but that it was his influence which made it acceptable. Jerome's successor, Augustine, gladly accepted the writing as an authentic letter of Paul.

References to the General Epistles are less frequent than to the previous writings. From very early in the second century, however, 1 Peter and 1 John were known and used, and there seem to have been no questions raised about either of them. It is not surprising that the other two letters of John were relatively late in appearing. Their length did not contribute to citations of them by writers, and 3 John, especially, was not the type of writing that could be widely used in the situation of the churches during those years. However, by the time of Irenaeus, 2 John seems to have achieved a firm place in the list of writings, and it would probably bring along with it 3 John. By the time of Origen, both of these smaller letters were known, although they still remained in his disputed list.

The situation of 2 Peter is much more doubtful. There seem to be no early references to it. Origen included it in his list of doubtful writings, and this may be the first clear reference to the work. However, its close association with the letter of 1 Peter quickly brought it into the accepted list during the subsequent decades.

The letter of Jude was known by Tertullian and Clement of Alexandria by the end of the second century. This writing proved valuable in combating later heresies and evidently was widely used after A.D. 200. It is true that both Origen and Eusebius placed it in their disputed list, but this status may have been due to its brevity and its citation of noncanonical Jewish writings.

The letter of James seems to have been slow in gaining a place in the life of the church. Since its contents were not such as would be highly valued and useful in conflict, this may account for its late appearance in writings. Origen placed it in his disputed list, and it was not widely used before the fourth century. Whether this reflects any doubt as to which James was its author cannot be determined.

The Book of Revelation had a varied history. Evidently it was accepted from the earliest days, both in the East and in the West. Both Justin Martyr and Papias seem to have been acquainted with it. However, the situation changed in the Eastern church about the close of the second century. A new heresy arose about the person and teachings of a man named Montanus, whose ideas centered in an emphasis on revelation and prophecy. He claimed that he and his followers received new revelations from God. The movement was oriented strongly toward an apocalyptic concept, the idea of a sudden and violent end brought about by God with the inauguration of his kingdom. This departure by Montanus brought all apocalyptic ideas into disrepute in the East. This meant that even the Book of Revelation fell from favor. It is true that such men as Clement of Alexandria and Origen might have retained it, but there was great hesitancy, not only in Alexandria but throughout the East. This is reflected in the fact that Eusebius placed the book in *both* his accepted and disputed lists. For the most part, the Eastern church put this book aside. It was one of the contributions of Athanasius that he was able to include the writing in his list of A.D. 367. It is likely that he became acquainted with the high value placed on the book in Rome during his exiles from Alexandria. He himself became convinced that it was authoritative and inspired, and thus he was able to include it. However, the book won its way in the East very slowly, and it was many years before it was accepted in such churches as the Syriac.

Summary

The development of the New Testament canon was a long process and not uniform in various parts of the Roman world. Many factors worked in the writing and collection of these documents. The fact that Hebrew Scriptures existed and were used from the first prepared the way for the later development of a second collection of strictly Christian writings. At first, the tradition of Jesus and his teaching was passed on in an oral form. Letters were written as occasion demanded. It was not long before the need was felt for written records of Jesus' teachings, and this was especially true as the gospel spread into the Greek-speaking world. As divergent opinions developed, there was the need for written authorities to which reference could be made to settle differences of belief and practice.

Mention has already been made of the motives that operated, probably unconsciously, in the selection of the materials that were eventually to make up the New Testament. It was not until the time of Irenaeus, late in the second century, that writers began consciously to discuss the various books that were used. The copying of larger New Testament manuscripts inevitably hastened the decision as to which books were most valuable, for it was necessary to decide which to include and which to exclude. This was the work of individual men and individual churches as God's Spirit led them to see the value of these writings in matters of faith and practice.

The church councils only acted at a later time, when the decisions had already been made in a practical way. A. H. McNeile wrote: "The books made their own place by a process which can be called, on the whole, the survival of the fittest, so that they were gradually set apart from all others as containing the sacred message of God."[12]

One important question remains to be asked. Is the canon of the New Testament closed? This may seem like a strange question, since we have our printed Bibles and they have contained the same books ever since the invention of printing. How could anyone imagine that any book might be omitted or any additional one included? Even Martin Luther, with his lack of appreciation of certain New Testament writings, had to include them, even though he did put them at the very end in a sort of appendix.

The answer to the question must be both yes and no. Yes, it is closed—because it seems impossible to suppose that anything could ever be added to our New Testament. I cannot imagine a kind of situation where the Christian community would ever permit this. Even if an unknown letter of Paul should be found and proved beyond doubt to be authentic, I do not believe that it would ever be accepted into the New Testament.

But the answer is also no. There has never been in the history of Christianity any group that has had the authority to close the canon. In a sense, this is something that could be done only by God. Thus, officially, it is still open, but, in practicality, it is closed. We have the New Testament in the form which we believe God originally intended, and we can have confidence that it presents the message that God has for his people today. Our task is to interpret it, understand it, practice it, and proclaim it. "Without adherence to the Canon, which—in the widest sense—witnesses to the history of Christ, faith in Christ in any church would become an illusion."[13]

Only a few of us know Greek. Therefore, the New Testament, in its original form, is not accessible to us. We are dependent upon translations, especially those into the English language. A survey of these translations now beckons us.

8

Translations of the Bible into English

Strange as it may seem to some people, our New Testament has not existed in an English translation since its beginning. Rather, the history of the development of the Bible into English has been one filled with discouragement, suffering, and even martyrdom. For some centuries, the church did not want the Bible in the language of the people. It was believed that only the clergy had the ability and the right to interpret Scripture. So long as the people knew the Scripture only in the interpretation placed upon it by the official clergy, the church could remain in control of them. A danger was seen if the Bible could be read and interpreted by the common people. Of course, for a long time, few people had the ability to read. However, we can look back and see the tragedy of what was being done. God intended his Word for all people, not for a select few—and the Holy Spirit gives to all the ability to interpret. The story of the translation of the Bible into English is the struggle to make it possible for all people to read for themselves.

Prior to the King James Version

There were some early efforts to make portions of the Bible available to the people in their own language. The best known of these were the poems by Caedmon, the Psalms translated by Aldhelm, and the efforts by Bede to translate portions of the New Testament. The Lindisfarne Gospels are a Latin copy of the Gospels with a literal translation written between the lines in English, copied about the year 1000.

But the credit for the most extensive translation into English, prior to the invention of printing, must go to John Wycliffe (c. 1330–1384). He believed that the Bible was the one rule of faith and practice. Since each person was responsible to God and responsible for obeying God's law, it was necessary that each person have the opportunity to read God's law, the Bible, in his own language. Thus, Wycliffe set about the task of translating the Bible and making it accessible through a group of traveling preachers who were devoted to his principles. Wycliffe's Bible appeared in two versions, the earlier one dated between 1380 and 1384. It was based on the Latin Vulgate, and no attempt seems to have been made to work with the original languages of the Bible. The earlier version was a literal translation of the Latin, while the later edition was a more idiomatic translation. By idiomatic, we mean that the attempt was made to translate the ideas or meaning, rather than give a word-by-word wooden rendering. Although copies of the Wycliffe Bible had to be made by hand, a large number of them were copied and the work of Wycliffe was quite influential in England.[1]

Credit for the first printed English New Testament goes to William Tyndale (1494–1536). Tyndale was a highly educated man with a great knowledge of languages. It is claimed that he knew Greek, Latin, Hebrew, French, Spanish, Italian, and German, as well as his native English. This gave him the ability to go back to the original Hebrew and Greek in his efforts to translate. At a rather early age he sensed the need for the Bible in the language of the people. It is claimed that in conversation with a learned man of the day, he expressed the purpose that through his efforts a boy driving a plow would know more of the Scripture than the learned man who seemed more interested in the decrees of the pope than in the Bible.[2] It soon became evident to Tyndale that there was no possibility of doing his work in England. Therefore, he fled to Germany where the political and religious climate was somewhat more acceptable. Although he began his work at Cologne, he was driven from that city and finally arrived in Worms, where his first complete New Testament was finished in 1536. Copies were immediately shipped to England. Actually, it was more of a smuggling operation, as copies shipped in were hidden in merchandise that was being sent from Germany to England.

Tyndale's work did not meet with approval on the part of the church officials. Tunstall (Tonstall), Bishop of London, did everything he could to prevent the shipment of the New Testament into England and to destroy the copies that did arrive. All the copies he could acquire were burned (and this was not to be the last time that public burning of Bibles took place). The bishop entered into an arrangement with a friend of Tyndale to buy a large number of the copies as they arrived in England, not realizing that the money he paid was being used to print up even more copies. It was stated that the bishop thought he had God by the toe, when in reality he had the devil by the fist.[3] Opposition to Tyndale became fierce, and it was to a large extent a personal matter. Although there was more opposition to the man than to his work, his work was subject to seizure and destruction. In May 1535, Tyndale was kidnaped from Antwerp, Belgium, where he was living. On 6 October 1536, he was strangled and burned at the stake, dying with the cry on his lips, "Lord, open the King of England's eyes."[4] What he did not know was that already there was a Bible in English being used with the permission of the king.

Although Tyndale was martyred because of his insistence that the Bible must be available in the language of the people, his influence has continued to the present time. J. Isaacs said of his work:

> Tindale's honesty, sincerity, and scrupulous integrity, his simple directness, his magical simplicity of phrase, his modest music, have given an authority to his wording that has imposed itself on all later versions. With all the tinkering to which the New Testament has been subject, Tindale's version is still the basis in phrasing, rendering, vocabulary,

rhythm, and often in music as well. Nine-tenths of the Authorized New Testament is still Tindale, and the best is still his.[5]

Since the Authorized Version lies at the base of the American Standard Version and the Revised Standard Version, it can be seen that the work of Tyndale has been largely preserved.

The fifty years following the death of Tyndale saw a flurry of interest in an English-language Bible. Myles Coverdale (1488–1569) had been an assistant to Tyndale, and he was persuaded to produce an English version of the Bible. This is known as the Coverdale Bible and was printed in 1535, the first complete Bible in English. Dedicated to King Henry VIII, it evidently was circulated with his approval. Coverdale was not the scholar that Tyndale was. He did not have the ability to use Hebrew and Greek, and thus it was claimed that his Bible was translated from the German and Latin. However, he made much use of Tyndale's translation for those parts which Tyndale had completed, which included all of the New Testament and parts of the Old.

In 1537, the Matthew's Bible appeared. It was prepared by John Rogers, and it had the king's license. Rogers had been a friend of Tyndale, and his Bible was primarily a revision of Tyndale's work.

The next important edition of the English Bible was the Great Bible (1539). It received this name because of its size, measuring 16½ by 11 inches. The intention was that it would replace the Coverdale and Matthew's Bibles. Times had changed in England since the days of Tyndale. In some areas of England it was now required that each church secure an English Bible and chain it to the desk so that it might be there for members to read. Since the Great Bible was prepared by Coverdale and was a revision of the Matthew's Bible, its ultimate origin was the work of Tyndale. The Great Bible was the first one which can properly be called an authorized version. On the title page appears the notice that it was appointed to be read in the churches.

The political history of England soon changed. After the death of Edward VI in 1553, Mary, Queen of Scots, became the ruler.

She brought back the Catholic influence, and many of the leading men of the Reformation in England either fled the country or were executed. Among those who fled were a number who settled in Geneva, where they found a friendly atmosphere, and it was from this city that the 1560 Geneva Bible came. Again, this New Testament was based to a large extent on the New Testament of Tyndale. Words for which there were no equivalent in the original language were printed in italics. This Bible was quite popular and soon became the most commonly used Bible by English-speaking Protestants. The Geneva Bible contained notes that were to prove offensive to many because they were thoroughly Calvinistic in tone. This is quite understandable since Geneva was the home of Calvin. Thus, although the Bible appealed to those who were Presbyterian in leaning, it was felt to be false by many who did not share this inclination.

As a result, the Church of England believed a new translation must be made which could compete with the Geneva Bible. This work was done under the leadership of a number of bishops and is known as the Bishops' Bible (1568). It was really a revision of the Great Bible, and the revisers were instructed "to use the Great Bible as their basis, and depart from it only where it did not accurately represent the original."[6] It was decreed that this Bible was to be placed in every church where possible, thus replacing the Great Bible, although it was never formally approved by the queen. According to Bruce, the Bishops' Bible did not measure up to the standard and quality of the Geneva Bible, which was the better translation.[7] While the Bishops' Bible did not receive royal approval, it was an authorized version so far as the Church of England was concerned. Thus, it stands in the list of authorized versions of the New Testament.

From the King James Version to the American Standard Version

The next authorized version was what is commonly known as the King James Version. In 1604, James VI convened a conference of churchmen at Hampton Court, at which he asked the assembled group to state anything which they thought wrong in the church. The major result of the conference was the proposal by John Reynolds, president of Corpus Christi College, Oxford, that there be a new translation of the Bible, because the ones produced during the reigns of Henry VIII and Edward VI were corrupt and not true to the original. The resolution adopted read:

> That a translation be made of the whole Bible, as consonant as can be to the original Hebrew and Greek; and this to be set out and printed, without any marginal notes, and only to be used in all Churches of England in time of divine service.[8]

This met with the enthusiastic approval of the king, who claimed that he had never seen a good translation into English and he believed the Geneva Bible to be the worst. Some forty-seven of the leading Bible scholars of England were enlisted for the task of translation. They were instructed to use the Bishops' Bible as the basis for their work, and changes were to be made only when the committee felt them necessary. The Greek text used in the translation of the New Testament was basically the text of Erasmus. The scholars did an excellent job of translating, and probably no translation ever made has equaled the version of 1611 in language, style, and dignity. This is one reason that it has retained its popularity through the centuries. The translators saw their task to be that of making a good translation better. They did not criticize the ones which had gone before, but they believed they were to make a translation which would serve as the one to be used—and the only one to be used—in the church.

However, the King James Version did not meet with immediate success, and it is hard for us to realize that for many years there was bitter opposition to this translation. It differed from the versions with which people were familiar, and they were reluctant to give up the readings which they had come to know and love. It was only throughout a period of almost half a century that the translation came to take its place as the basic one used by the people—and it went through many revisions (1613, 1629, 1638, 1762,

1769). Thus, although the King James Version which we know today differs in many ways from the edition that was published in 1611, it has been the standard for English translation ever since it first appeared. But many things have worked since that time to make the need for new translations a reality.

As noted in the earlier discussion of textual study, the years following 1611 saw many advancements in the study of the New Testament. Large numbers of new, older, and better manuscripts were discovered. The study of these indicated that the late text on which the King James Version was based was not the best and most reliable text of the New Testament. In addition, much study was devoted to the Greek language itself. There was a far better understanding of the meaning of the Greek than could have been available in 1611. Beyond all this was the fact that the English language was in the process of change. As is true with any living language, there were constant changes, so that what was contemporary and clear in 1611 would not have been so two centuries later.

Thus, by 1870, forces were beginning to move which led to the decision that a revision should be made. The result of this was the Revised Version of 1881. In 1870, committees were appointed to begin the revision of the King James Version, although it was not the intention to make a new translation. The instructions were "To introduce as few alterations as possible into the Text of the Authorized Version consistently with faithfulness."[9] The translators were helped in their work when Westcott and Hort made available to them their text of the Greek New Testament, which was published at almost the same time as the New Testament of the Revised Version. Their Greek text thus served as the basic text used by the translators, and it was a text which was far superior to that which had been available in 1611.

The committee charged with the responsibility of making this revision was assisted by a committee of American scholars. The original hope was that a revision could be produced which could be published in identical form and at the same time on both sides of the Atlantic. However, this did not prove possible. The American committee continued to work after 1881 to produce a version that would be more acceptable to people in the United States. The result was the American Standard Version of 1901. While in essence the two versions are the same, there are a number of variations which relate to the differences in the language and culture of the two countries.

Since the American Standard Version has had more influence in the United States, it is well to comment on it, rather than on the Revised Version. It has been claimed that the American Standard Version is the most accurate version ever to be made in English, and this is probably true. This is the highest recommendation that can be made for the translation, but, at the same time, is its greatest drawback. For the student who wishes to know in the best possible way what the original text said, without having access to that original, no other translation is its equal. However, for that very reason it is not very readable, and it is too literal to be good English. Thus, the American Standard Version never achieved the popularity which had been hoped for it.

Before turning to the many translations which have appeared in the twentieth century, a brief word should be said about Catholic translations. For a long time, the standard Catholic translation of the New Testament was the Rheims New Testament (1582). It was based on the Latin Vulgate and was revised by Richard Challoner between 1749 and 1772. More recent Catholic translations include that of Ronald A. Knox (1945), the New American Bible (1941, revised 1970), and the Jerusalem Bible (1966).

After the American Standard Version

The twentieth century has seen an abundance (some might say an overabundance) of English translations.[10] In 1903, Richard F. Weymouth published *The New Testament in Modern Speech*. It seems that he attempted to put the New Testament into a form of modern English that might be described as "dignified." Weymouth gave careful attention to grammar.

The next significant translation is that of James Moffatt. *The*

New Testament: A New Translation appeared in 1913, followed in 1928 by a translation of the entire Bible. It was a tremendous undertaking for one man to translate and publish the entire Bible, using the original Hebrew and Greek languages. Moffatt's translation is quite idiomatic, and some of his idioms sound rather strange to American readers. His work was popular, as it was aimed at the general reader in an effort to make the Bible live and be more understandable. Unfortunately for the lasting success of Moffatt's work, the New Testament was based on the Greek text of von Soden, a text which has not stood the test of time. In addition, Moffatt took liberty with the arrangement of material, which is somewhat confusing to the reader.

Edgar J. Goodspeed (1923) published *The New Testament: An American Translation.* J. M. Powis Smith translated the Old Testament, and the entire work was published as *The Complete Bible: An American Translation,* in 1927. This translation was designed for an American readership, much as Moffatt's had been intended for a British audience.

In 1924, Helen Barrett Montgomery published her translation, the *Centenary Translation of the New Testament.* This is perhaps the only noted translation of the New Testament by a woman.

One of the striking translations of the New Testament was that of Charles B. Williams, *The New Testament in the Language of the People,* first published in 1937. Williams sought to express in English the exact shade of meaning of the Greek verbs. It may be that his effort in this direction is the most successful ever done.

One of the major translations of the twentieth century is the Revised Standard Version. The New Testament of this version was first published in 1946, and the entire Bible in 1952. (The New Testament portion was revised in 1971.) A committee of thirty-two men was appointed to carry out this revision of the American Standard Version. We must note that this was a revision, not a new translation. As much as some might wish the committee had been charged with the responsibility of making a new translation, this was not their instruction. Once more, the idea was that as few changes as possible should be made. Thus, the Revised Standard

Version stands in the same line as the American Standard Version, the Revised Version, the King James Version, the Bishops' Bible, and the Great Bible—all of them to a large extent dependent upon the work of William Tyndale.

The Revised Standard Version met with violently different reactions. Many acclaimed it as the best translation ever made, others insisted that it was the work of the devil. Copies were burned, especially after the Old Testament translation was published. It may be that we are still too close to the publication of this translation to make a fair assessment of it. We must remember how long it took the King James Version to win out over its opponents. F. F. Bruce states this:

> To a large extent, the revisers have succeeded in satisfying the requirement of those mid-twentieth century readers who look for an English Bible which will do for today and tomorrow what the A. V. did for the seventeenth and following centuries. [11]

He also notes that no modern version of the Bible "comes so near as the R. S. V. does to making the all-purpose provision which the A. V. made for so many years." [12] The Revised Standard Version has been officially approved by the Roman Catholic Church for study, and the version which contains the expanded Apocrypha has been approved by authorities of the Eastern Orthodox Church.

In 1947, the first volume of J. B. Phillips's translation of the New Testament was published. This portion contained the letters of Paul. A free rendering of the original, it was immensely popular. Many would contend that it is more a paraphrase than a translation. However, Phillips's intention was to make the Scripture speak to the person of today in the same way that the Greek spoke to the people of the first century. This necessitated freedom in translation. His entire New Testament was published in 1958: *The New Testament in Modern English.*

Another translation that has received some degree of popularity is *The Berkeley Version of the New Testament* (1945). The entire Bible of this translation was published in 1959. The New Testament was translated by Gerrit Verkuyl, and the Old Testament was the work of a group of about twenty scholars.

The Amplified Bible was published in 1965, and it is designed to give the reader a variety of possibilities in translation. Alternate renderings are placed in parentheses in the text. Thus the reader has the benefit of a number of possible meanings as he studies a particular verse.

The year 1966 saw the publishing of *Today's English Version,* also called *Good News for Modern Man.* The New Testament was translated by Robert G. Bratcher. The complete *Good News Bible* was published in 1976. This Bible attempts to present the Scripture in contemporary language, and the New Testament, especially, quickly became a popular translation.

The next major translation was the *New English Bible.* The New Testament was published in 1961, and the entire Bible in 1970. From the beginning, this was not intended as a revision. Instead, the effort was to make a completely new translation from the original languages without the use of any intervening English version. Not only were biblical scholars enlisted for this translation, but also a committee of advisors was used for literary and style questions. The intention was to make a translation that would be suitable for use both in private and public worship services. The translation is generally recognized as quite good, but we American readers will find a number of expressions which sound strange to our ears.

The *New American Standard New Testament* was published in 1960, and the entire Bible in 1971. As the name implies, it is a revision of the American Standard Version of 1901. An effort has been made to make the language of the American Standard Version more readable. Much work has been expended in seeking to make the Greek verb tenses clear in the English translation. At the same time, the editors have sought to keep the exactness of the 1901 version.

The Living Bible was published in 1971. Actually this is a paraphrase executed by Kenneth N. Taylor, and was originally intended for his own children. While it is widely used, there are many places where the editor has introduced, into the text, ideas of his own which cannot be supported by the Scripture itself. This is always a danger when a translation is made by one individual, since there are certain safeguards present when a work is done by a committee.

The final translation to be mentioned is the *New International Version.* The New Testament was published in 1973 and the entire Bible in 1978. It was sponsored by the New York Bible Society and written in what can be thought of as the language of the common person. It may be too recent for one to give any opinion about its ultimate popularity or value.

Summary

What is to be done with such a great variety of translations? The reader will note that no attempt has been made in this survey to rate these translations as to which is the best or which is the poorest. Such an effort would require far more space than can be allotted to this portion of the study. In addition, excellent works are available which undertake such a task.[13] What has been attempted is to acquaint the reader with the vast variety of translations which is available and something of the background out of which each translation has come.

It is probably true that there is no such thing as a poor translation of the Bible, and it is also true that there is no perfect translation. We would not suggest that translators have been inspired in the same manner as were the original writers. However, we can see that God's redemptive work can be understood from any of the translations. Thus, in the final analysis, the crucial question may not be which translation one should use. Rather, any serious reader of the Bible should have more than one translation.

Probably most readers will want a copy of the King James Version. One should probably also possess one of the standard twentieth-century translations, such as the Revised Standard Version, the *New English Bible,* and *New American Standard Bible,* or the *New International Version.* In addition to these, the reader will want one of the modern language translations.

Then he or she should regularly compare the translations of the passage being studied. Such a procedure will provide a source of enlightenment in the study of God's Word. Which translations one should use is primarily a matter of personal choice, as what might be best for one person will not necessarily be so for another. What seems best to me may not be as helpful for someone else. But do have a number of translations and use them. In this way, God can speak to you in fresh terms—revealing himself and his purpose to you.

Kubo and Specht suggest three criteria to be used in choosing a translation. The first relates to the text from which the translation is made. It is important that it be the most reliable text possible. The second is the accuracy of the translation. Does it present carefully the message of the original? The third is the quality of its English. It is important that the version be clear.[14]

While at times the large number of translations may appear confusing to us, we should rejoice that the Bible is so readily available. No one of us would want to go back to the early sixteenth century where the Bible could not be found in English. Perhaps we take our good fortune too much for granted. People in that former day were willing to sacrifice their lives for the privilege which we have. Such a realization should make us more diligent in the study of Scripture. God speaks to us in its pages. Our study of the development of the Greek text, the growth of the canon of the New Testament, and the history of the translation of the New Testament into English should have led us to a deeper appreciation of the New Testament and a determination to be more faithful students of it. But the ultimate goal must be that we seek to put into practice what God has taught us from it. Unless we do that, all of our efforts must be in vain.

Endnotes

Chapter 1

[1]A. T. Robertson, *An Introduction to the Textual Criticism of the New Testament* (Nashville, Tennessee: Broadman Press, 1925), p. 74.
[2]Complete lists of the papyri can be found in Bruce M. Metzger, *The Text of the New Testament* (New York: Oxford University Press, second edition, 1968), pp. 247–256; and in Kurt Aland, et al, editors, *Novum Testamentum Graece* (Stuttgart: Deutsche Bibelstiftung, 26th edition, 1979), pp. 684–689. In addition, F. G. Kenyon, Third Edition Revised and Augmented by A. W. Adams, *The Text of the Greek Bible* (London: Duckworth, 1975), pp. 67–77, lists and describes most of the important papyri.
[3]Robertson, p. 85.
[4]Metzger, p. 57.
[5]A list of all the important uncial manuscripts can be found in Metzger, pp. 42–61, and a list of all the uncials in Aland, pp. 689–702.
[6]More detailed lists of minuscule manuscripts can be found in Metzger, pp. 61–66; Kenyon, pp. 104–110; Aland, pp. 702–710.
[7]Metzger, p. 68.

Chapter 2

[1]"For Greek copies indeed we are indebted to your Holiness, who sent us most kindly from the Apostolic Library very ancient codices, both of the Old and the New Testament; which have aided us very much in this undertaking." Quoted in Bruce M. Metzger, *The Text of the New Testament* (New York: Oxford University Press, second edition, 1968), p. 98.
[2]Metzger, p. 99.
[3]Metzger, pp. 101–102.
[4]Variant readings are manuscript readings which differ from the reading which

the editor has placed in his text. The term will be used frequently in this writing without further explanation.

[5]A. T. Robertson, *An Introduction to the Textual Criticism of the New Testament* (Nashville, Tennessee: Broadman Press, 1925), p. 100.

[6]Metzger, p. 106.

[7]Metzger, p. 109.

[8]"The author believes that he has retrieved (except in very few places) the true exemplar of Origen, which was the standard to the most learned of the *Fathers*, at the time of the Council of Nice and two centuries after. And he is sure that the Greek and Latin MSS., by their mutual assistance, do so settle the original text to the smallest nicety, as cannot be performed now in any *classic* author whatever; and that out of a labyrinth of thirty thousand various readings, that crowd the pages of our present best editions, all put upon equal credit, to the offence of many good persons, this clue so leads and extricates us, that there will scarce be two hundred out of so many thousands that can deserve the least consideration." Quoted in Frederic G. Kenyon, *Handbook to the Textual Criticism of the New Testament* (Grand Rapids, Michigan: Wm. B. Eerdmans Publishing Company, second edition, 1953), p. 277.

[9]J. Harold Greenlee, *Introduction to New Testament Textual Criticism* (Grand Rapids, Michigan: Wm. B. Eerdmans Publishing Company, 1964), p. 60.

[10]Kirsopp Lake, *The Text of the New Testament* (New York: Edwin S. Gorham, 1903), p. 61.

[11]Metzger, p. 114.

[12]Marvin R. Vincent, *A History of the Textual Criticism of the New Testament* (New York: The Macmillan Company, 1899), p. 92.

[13]Vincent, p. 101.

[14]Robertson, p. 26.

[15]Vincent, pp. 102–103.

[16]Brooke Foss Westcott and Fenton John Anthony Hort, *The New Testament in the Original Greek* (New York: Harper & Brothers, 1882), ii, 13.

[17]A critical apparatus lists, in the margin or at the bottom of the page, variant readings with notations which identify the manuscripts which contain those readings.

[18]Westcott and Hort, pp. 13–14.

Chapter 3

[1]Bruce M. Metzger, *The Text of the New Testament* (New York: Oxford University Press, second edition, 1968), p. 17.

[2]Metzger, pp. 17–18.

[3]Metzger, p. 16.

[4]Metzger, p. 15.

[5]This type of error is called *homoeoteleuton*.

[6]This type of error is called *dittography*.

[7]A. T. Robertson, *An Introduction to the Textual Criticism of the New Testament* (Nashville, Tennessee: Broadman Press, 1925), p. 154.

[8]Metzger, p. 195.
[9]Metzger, p. 195.
[10]Robertson, p. 159.

Chapter 4

[1]Vincent Taylor, *The Text of the New Testament* (London: Macmillan & Co Ltd, second edition, 1963), p. 4.
[2]Brooke Foss Westcott and Fenton John Anthony Hort, *The New Testament in the Original Greek* (New York: Harper & Brothers, 1882), ii, 31.
[3]Westcott and Hort, ii, 134–35.
[4]Westcott and Hort, ii, 122.
[5]The Western non-interpolations are in Matt. 27:49; Luke 22:19–20; 24:3, 6, 12, 36, 40, 51, 52.
[6]Westcott and Hort, ii, 131–32.
[7]A. T. Robertson, *An Introduction to the Textual Criticism of the New Testament* (Nashville, Tennessee: Broadman Press, 1925), p. 161.
[8]Westcott and Hort, ii, 25.
[9]Westcott and Hort, ii, 2.
[10]Burnett Hillman Streeter, *The Four Gospels* (London: Macmillan and Co., Limited, 1951), pp. 26–148.
[11]Streeter, pp. 91–107.
[12]Bruce M. Metzger, *Chapters in the History of the New Testament Textual Criticism* (Grand Rapids, Michigan: Wm. B. Eerdmans, 1963), pp. 42–72.
[13]F. G. Kenyon, *The Text of the Greek Bible*, Third Edition Revised and Augmented by A. W. Adams (London: Duckworth, 1975), pp. 212–13.
[14]Kenyon, p. 253.
[15]Benjamin B. Warfield, *An Introduction to Textual Criticism of the New Testament* (London: Hodder and Stoughton, 1886), p. 156.
[16]Eldon Jay Epp, "The Twentieth Century Interlude in New Testament Textual Criticism," *Journal of Biblical Literature*, 93 (September, 1974), 386–414.
[17]Epp, p. 390.
[18]Epp, p. 392.
[19]Epp, p. 405.
[20]J. N. Birdsall, "The New Testament Text," *The Cambridge History of the Bible*, volume 1, *From the Beginnings to Jerome*, edited by P. R. Ackroyd and C. F. Evans (Cambridge: University Press, 1970), pp. 308–309.
[21]Epp, p. 404.
[22]Birdsall, p. 317.
[23]Kenyon, p. 254.

Chapter 5

[1]Information on variant readings is derived for the most part from Kurt Aland, et al, editors, *The Greek New Testament* (New York: United Bible Societies, third edition, 1975).

Chapter 6

[1]Alexander Souter, *The Text and Canon of the New Testament*, revised by C. S. C. Williams (London: Gerald Duckworth & Co., Ltd., 1954), pp. 141–42.

[2]A. H. McNeile, *An Introduction to the Study of the New Testament*, second edition revised by C. S. C. Williams (Oxford: Clarendon Press, 1953), p. 311.

[3]H. F. D. Sparks, *The Formation of the New Testament* (New York: Philosophical Library, 1953), p. 12.

[4]Brooke Foss Westcott, *A General Survey of the History of the Canon of the New Testament*, sixth edition (Grand Rapids, Michigan: Baker Book House, 1980), p. 6.

[5]Robert M. Grant, *The Formation of the New Testament* (New York: Harper & Row, Publishers, 1965), p. 25.

[6]Edgar J. Goodspeed, *The Meaning of Ephesians* (Chicago: The University of Chicago Press, 1933), pp. 3–17.

[7]John Knox, *Philemon Among the Letters of Paul* (New York: Abingdon Press, 1959), pp. 71–108.

[8]William Barclay, *The Making of the Bible* (New York: Abingdon Press, 1961), p. 69.

[9]Grant, pp. 81–83.

[10]Souter, p. 140.

[11]McNeile, p. 314.

[12]Hans von Campenhausen, *The Formation of the Christian Bible*, translated by J. A. Baker (Philadelphia: Fortress Press, 1972), p. 121.

[13]Campenhausen, pp. 148–167.

Chapter 7

[1]Robert M. Grant, *The Formation of the New Testament* (New York: Harper & Row, Publishers, 1965), p. 84.

[2]Adolf Jülicher, *An Introduction to the New Testament*, translated by Janet Penrose Ward (London: Smith, Elder, & Co., 1904), p. 484.

[3]Irenaeus, *Against Heresies*, III, xi, 8. The Rev. Alexander Roberts and James Donaldson, editors, *The Ante-Nicene Fathers*, American reprint of the Edinburgh edition (Grand Rapids, Michigan: Wm. B. Eerdmans Publishing Company, 1950), i, 428.

[4]Hans von Campenhausen, *The Formation of the Christian Bible*, translated by J. A. Baker (Philadelphia: Fortress Press, 1972). p. 172.

[5]C. F. D. Moule, *The Birth of the New Testament* (New York: Harper & Row, Publishers, 1962), pp. 187 f.

[6]Campenhausen, p. 203.

[7]Morton Smith, *The Secret Gospel* (New York: Harper & Row, Publishers, 1973).

[8]A. C. Sundberg, Jr., "Muratorian Fragment," *The Interpreter's Dictionary of the Bible*, Supplementary Volume (Nashville: Abingdon, 1976), pp. 609–610.

[9]Brooke Foss Westcott, *A General Survey of the History of the Canon of the New Testament*, sixth edition (Grand Rapids, Michigan: Baker Book House, 1980), p. 218.

[10]Jülicher, p. 508.

[11]Souter, p. 171.

[12]A. H. McNeile, *An Introduction to the Study of the New Testament*, second edition revised by C. S. C. Williams (Oxford: Clarendon Press, 1953), p. 372.

[13]Campenhausen, p. 333.

Chapter 8

[1]It is not necessary to go into so much detail in this portion of our study since there are good books dealing with the English Bible which the reader can use. Among these are F. F. Bruce, *History of the Bible in English* (New York: Oxford University Press, third edition, 1978); Sakae Kubo and Walter Specht, *So Many Versions?* (Grand Rapids, Michigan: Zondervan Publishing House, 1975); Herbert Gordon May, *Our English Bible in the Making: The Word of Life in Living Language* (Philadelphia: Westminster Press, revised edition, 1965); Ira Maurice Price, *The Ancestry of Our English Bible*, third edition edited by William A. Irwin and Allen P. Wikgren (New York: Harper & Brothers, 1956); Jack P. Lewis, *The English Bible from KJV to NIV* (Grand Rapids, Michigan: Baker Book House, 1981).

[2]John Foxe, *Foxe's Book of Martyrs*, Edited and Abridged by G. A. Williamson (Boston: Little, Brown and Company, 1965), p. 121.

[3]Foxe, p. 90.

[4]Bruce, p. 52.

[5]J. Isaacs, "The Sixteenth Century English Versions," *The Bible in Its Ancient and English Versions*, edited by H. Wheeler Robinson (Oxford: Clarendon Press, 1940), p. 160.

[6]Bruce, p. 93.

[7]Bruce, p. 94.

[8]Bruce, p. 96.

[9]Bruce, p. 137.

[10]Detailed discussion of twentieth-century translations can be found in the book by Kudo and Specht. This book gives a critical appraisal of each of the translations, citing both the strengths and weaknesses of each.

[11]Bruce, p. 194.

[12]Bruce, p. 203.

[13]See especially the works by Bruce, Kudo and Specht, and Lewis.

[14]Kubo and Specht, pp. 203–207.

Index

157